New Mexico's Tasty Traditions

Author: Sharon Niederman

Editors: Emily Drabanski, Penny Landay, Walter K. Lopez

Design & Production: Bette Brodsky

Publisher: Ethel Hess

Library of Congress PCN Number: 2010934270
ISBN: 978-1-934480-05-2
Printed in Korea

Cover photo: *Sopyn's roadside fruit stand on N.M. 68, south of Taos,
offers an abundance of fresh fruits and vegetables.*

Contents photo: *The women of Springer sell pies on the Saturday
morning of the Colfax County Fair.*

New Mexico's Tasty Traditions

recollections, recipes and photos

SHARON NIEDERMAN

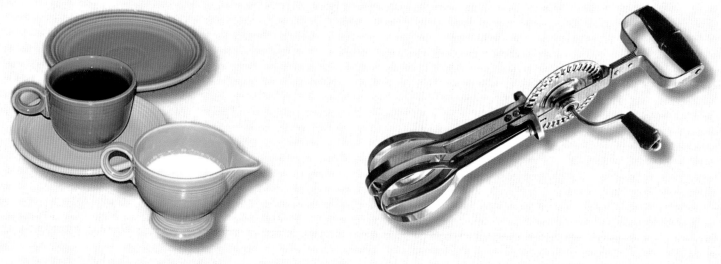

CONTENTS

My first taste of New Mexican cuisine was not auspicious. Visiting Albuquerque to attend a conference, I stopped for lunch at a highly recommended downtown eatery, M & J's Sanitary Tortilla Factory. I ordered the special of the day. I don't remember if it was smothered in red or green chile, but the dish was so hot I grabbed my glass of water and started screaming, "What is wrong with this food? I can't believe they actually charge money for this!"

A year later, following my move to New Mexico, I was sitting in the same restaurant, happily chowing down on M & J's legendary fare, and the same waitress who'd served me the previous year came by. "I remember you," she said. "Look at you now!" We both had a good laugh.

Since that first lunch almost 30 years ago, not only have I learned to love chile, but our state's cuisine has also become one of my greatest passions. My others are writing and traveling. So with great pleasure, I have traveled New Mexico's back roads to gather information for the many stories about the state's tasty traditions that I've written for dozens of publications.

It is with great joy that I've visited with chefs in restaurants and cooks in their homes. I enjoy collecting recipes and the related stories—told in voices both genuine and

Above—Bridge Street in Las Vegas offers several places to sample regional cuisine. Estella's Café, seen here in the center of the block, has served tasty red and green chile for three generations.

Opposite—Fresh-picked produce, harvested at its peak, is available at farmers markets throughout the state. Sunny's Garden at Rainbow Ranch in Folsom uses simple organic principles, drawing water from a pond fed by an aboveground, wet stretch of the "Dry Cimarron" riverbed to water the vegetables.

Grab a microbrew or order a house-made root beer float at Three Rivers Eatery & Brewery in Farmington, the place to stop after fishing in the San Juan River.

generous. I love the wisdom, humor and good sense that develop in this place where people simply "use what they have." Often that's not much, as measured by the outside world.

I relish the stories that seem to rise out of the landscape, demanding to be told. I keep a little notepad in the car, so I can scribble ideas inspired along the miles, and my camera is always at my side. I am always prepared to stop, jump out and focus my lens on a gathering, an interesting sign or a makeshift roadside market.

To know New Mexico, you must taste its flavors—the heat of its chiles, the sweetness of its honey and the ripeness of its pecans. In these flavors are the tastes of the sun, the wind and the waters that flow in the acequias. Every lovingly prepared dish reflects the weathered wisdom of unbroken tradition and the strong hands that nurture and respect the land.

New Mexico's Tasty Traditions: Recollections, Recipes and Photos is the result of some of my many culinary adventures. I have visited a ranch kitchen in Harding County (pop. 900) to taste melt-in-your-mouth *bizcochitos*, served homemade pie and *potica* bread in Raton, savored pungent chile dishes at classic cafés in El Rito and La Mesa, and gathered at dawn with the women of Isleta Pueblo as they prepare bread loaves for the *horno*.

Nature's bounty has also added richness to my own recipes. I have foraged for wild plums, dandelions and wild rose hips. I have even made chokecherry jam. I have caught and cooked trout in Cimarrón Canyon.

With gusto, I have judged cooking competitions: Scobie hot sauce contests, the New Mexico State Fair Green Chile contest and Dutch-oven cook-offs in Mountainair and Glenwood.

I am grateful to the farmers and ranchers who produce what stocks my freezer and pantry: local organic lamb and beef, chile, corn, beans and a variety of fresh produce. It's always fun to visit with the growers who share their harvest at the state's many farmers markets.

Some of my happiest days have been spent at New Mexico's fiestas and festivals. I love tasting food from the vendors and listening to music that reflects the state's many cultures. I get a kick out of watching the young and old gather at parades, processions and traditional dances. For me this is pure joy.

I hope you will experience some of that joy as you read *New Mexico's Tasty Traditions: Recollections, Recipes and Photos*. Let this book be your guide to exploring the flavors of the state, in your own kitchen and at cafés on the road. I hope that you never become so busy that you can't get away to celebrate the harvest and taste the wine.

Ranch children, like this youngster at the Colfax County Fair, shower their show animals with care and affection, hoping to bring home a blue ribbon. They learn to be responsible, to get their chores done and to understand that their animals depend on them.

Enjoy and savor the stories within this book. I hope that the recipes inspire you to cook and share these New Mexico dishes with your friends and family.

—*Sharon Niederman*
August 2010
Raton, New Mexico

Above—*Rodeo princesses enjoy a well-earned barbecue lunch with all the fixin's at the Colfax County Fair in Springer.*

Opposite—*Some of the best red chile and other regional specialties can be found in "chow carts." Annette's Home Cooking, now closed, served fresh fry bread and Indian tacos just outside Taos Pueblo.*

Thre's no telling if Springer's annual cakewalk is New Mexico's last bona fide community contest of its kind, but where else can you find a numbered circle the size of a circus tent on a downtown street?

This cakewalk circle is not simply a temporary chalk design. Rather, it is painted on the street as clearly as the white lines designating parking spaces, and it stays bright all year-round, rekindling memories and piquing the interest of passersby.

Every year in August, on the Saturday morning of the annual Colfax County Fair, people from across northeastern New Mexico travel to Springer for a chance to win a tasty, homemade cake.

Springer is a quiet town of roughly 1,200 souls, many of them elderly. Most residents have homesteading and ranching in their backgrounds. Its name was long synonymous with the town's primary business, the state correctional boys' home, but even that institution of last resort has closed its doors, replaced by another incarceration facility.

Springer had its formal beginnings in 1879, taking its name from Frank Springer, influential lawyer of the Maxwell Land Grant Company. The Santa Fe Trail runs nearby, and several important trail landmarks are located in the vicinity. Springer Lake is a hot spot for landing northern pike. But at the cakewalk, everyone hopes to snag a deliciously sweet cake.

The Colfax County Fair is the biggest event of the year in Springer. The Methodist Church bazaar presented in the fall runs a distant second, though if the word got out about its red chile and Frito pies, who knows?

No one can say for certain how long Springer's cakewalk custom has been in place. Master of ceremonies Pete Pacheco says "more than twenty

Opposite—*The annual cakewalk at the Colfax County Fair in Springer is a time when families get together to have fun. Participants parade around the giant circle painted on the street until the music stops, hoping to win a cake.*

It's hard to say which is more fun—winning the prize or eating the cake. This young gal's pretty pink shirt matches the frosting on the cake.

years," while some participants more than 50 years old remember doing the cakewalk as children. Nevertheless, it remains a county fair highlight that brings generations together. Those who have moved to Albuquerque, Santa Fe, Angel Fire and beyond come home again for this special event. It's not unusual to see several generations of a family strolling the cakewalk together. The annual August gathering is marked on local calendars with as much definitive certainty as Thanksgiving or Christmas.

Here's how it works: For 25 cents, you buy a ticket that grants a chance at winning one of the three dozen or so big, scrumptious chocolate, coconut, cherry-cheese, spice, yellow and German chocolate cakes. They are baked and beautifully decorated by the wives, sisters, mothers and girlfriends of the Knights of Columbus. OK, so it's not like winning the lottery. But your odds of walking away as the day's big winner are a whole lot better.

Under any circumstances, the opportunity to dig into one of these fresh-baked confections would be a joy. On the sunny August morning of the cakewalk, however, anticipation builds as the dozens of cakes arrayed in the shadowy cool of the feed store/newspaper office reach a critical mass with an aroma reminiscent of every birthday cake you've ever wished on.

Everyone cues up to stand on one of the giant squares forming a circle in the street, as they daydream about winning the showiest and tastiest prize.

Tex-Mex music provides the beat from a tinny boom box in the middle of the circle as participants parade around the circuit, stepping on one numbered square at a time. If you are standing on the number that is drawn when the music stops, you win a cake. If the number drawn points to an empty square, more numbers are drawn until a winner materializes.

And what a cake! Your prize is hand-delivered by Colfax and Santa Fe County rodeo and fair queens, decked out in gleaming chartreuse, gold and red satin finery, while sporting big cowboy hats.

Whether you are 6 or 60, winning a cake for a quarter is a triumph worth remembering.

After the cakewalk, it's time to watch the festive parade on Maxwell Avenue. Then folks mosey over to the fairgrounds to eat barbecue, climb into the bleachers and enjoy the rodeo.

The cakewalk custom has made a long and astonishing journey from its origins in the South to this little northern New Mexico village. There are several interpretations of how the cakewalk tradition began. But one of the most common explanations is that while observing Seminole Indian processions, African slaves in Florida decided to embellish the Seminoles' native custom with their own style of movement. Their masters began holding Sunday dance competitions in which dancers actually mocked the high and fine manners of the folks who lived in the big houses by exaggerating their movements. The winner received a cake.

So popular were the Southern cakewalks that the dance style crossed over and was adapted by white folks themselves. The cakewalk's exaggerated movements and high stepping, which began as satire, became the first popular American dance to migrate from black to white culture. The music and movements of the cakewalk caught on, becoming elements of ragtime and minstrel shows. Some popular writers suggest that eventually the dance evolved into the Charleston, the Lindy Hop and, ultimately, break dancing.

This young winner is all smiles as she holds her prize.

Part of the fun of winning is getting your cake hand-delivered by the beautiful and accomplished county fair and rodeo queens. They happily deliver cakes with grins as wide as their cowboy hat brims.

Many people who grew up in small towns throughout New Mexico remember doing the cakewalk in the same manner as it is now done in Springer. They recall when suitors or would-be boyfriends manufactured elaborate schemes for winning the cake baked by a special girl.

Pacheco estimates that the cakewalk puts about $360 in Springer's Knights of Columbus treasury to be used for scholarships, Christmas groceries for the needy and other charitable activities. He enjoys keeping the custom going if only to see the smiles on the faces of youngsters when they win.

"It's nice to do something for the community," he says.

Christine Bernal, who grew up in Springer, left and returned home a few years ago. She is compiling a book of her favorite cake recipes for her children. When they were growing up, she offered them a choice between her apple walnut cake with buttermilk sauce and red velvet cake for their birthdays. A girlfriend gave her the apple walnut cake recipe, and the red velvet cake recipe came from Christine's mother, Esther Montoya.

Making these cakes is a wonderful reminder of Springer's sweetest tradition.

RECIPES

Christine Bernal's Apple Walnut Cake
(Serves 8–10)

    3 cups sifted flour
    1 teaspoon baking soda
    2 cups sugar
    1 teaspoon vanilla
    2 cups grated, unpared apples (Pink Lady,
        Gala or Fuji)
    1 cup sweetened, canned, flaked coconut
    3 eggs
    ¼ cup oil
    1 teaspoon cinnamon
    ¼ cup orange juice
    1 cup walnuts

Sift flour, baking soda and cinnamon.

Combine sugar, eggs, oil, vanilla and orange juice in a large bowl. Beat with an electric mixer until ingredients are well mixed.

Stir in the flour mixture. Fold in apples, walnuts and coconut.

Spoon into a well-oiled, heavy bundt pan. Bake at 350 degrees F for 1½ hours or until the top springs back.

Buttermilk Sauce and Decoration

    1 cup sugar
    ½ cup butter
    ½ teaspoon baking soda
    ½ cup buttermilk
    1–2 apples

Mix all ingredients except the apples. Cook over medium heat, stirring constantly, until the mixture comes to a boil, approximately 20 minutes.

Meanwhile, cut 1–2 apples into wedges. Wedge them into the center of the cake to form a flower.

Take a wooden skewer and punch numerous holes in the cake to better absorb the sauce. Pour buttermilk sauce over the cake. Serve.

The cakes baked by the wives, mothers, sisters and girlfriends of the Knights of Columbus stay cool inside the feed store during the cakewalk. Inside, the sweet aroma of dozens of fresh-baked chocolate, spice and coconut cakes is heavenly.

Christine Bernal's Red Velvet Cake
(Serves 8–10)

- ¼ lb. butter
- 2 eggs
- 2 ounces red food coloring
- 1 teaspoon salt
- 2 cups cake flour (must be cake flour)
- 1½ cups sugar
- 2 tablespoons cocoa (Christine prefers NesQuick.)
- 1 teaspoon vanilla
- 1 cup buttermilk
- 1½ teaspoons baking soda
- 1 teaspoon vinegar

Cream butter, sugar and eggs.

Make a paste of cocoa and food coloring. Add to the creamed mixture.

Mix salt with vanilla and buttermilk. Add buttermilk and cocoa mixtures to the flour, alternating each one. On the last folding, add baking soda and vinegar. Do not beat.

Bake 30 minutes at 350 degrees F.

Red Velvet Cake Frosting

- 5 tablespoons flour
- 1 cup whole milk
- 1 cup butter
- 1 cup granulated sugar
- 1 teaspoon vanilla

Add flour to milk. Boil until thick. Let the mixture stand at room temperature for a few hours, covered with wax paper.

Beat butter and sugar with vanilla using an electric mixer until all ingredients are creamy. Add the milk and flour mixture. Beat until fluffy. Frost the cake.

hose who lived, worked or grew up in the coal camps and mining towns dotting northern New Mexico and southern Colorado will remember the taste of a rich nut-and-fruit-filled loaf served during the Christmas season called *potica* bread (pronounced pah-TEET-zah). From Raton to Gallup, where it is known as *povitica* (po-vi-TEEK-a), and north to Pueblo, Colorado, this cake-like bread conjures up memories as sweet as its melt-in-the-mouth taste. Baked into every loaf are the warmth and traditions of the holiday season spent among cherished friends and family. The recipe, brought to the American West by Slavic miners, was gladly shared with Italian and Hispanic neighbors in mining communities.

While *potica* may be served at Easter, weddings, anniversaries, birthdays and confirmations, Christmas is the time to count on finding it. Dedicated *potica* baker Betty Antonucci of Raton, who was raised in Pueblo, says, "My mother made it for years. All the Italian people do. It was just always there at Christmas time. It can be used as a bread with the main course but is generally a dessert. It's very good served warm with hot butter. I like to serve it at Christmas time when somebody comes over." Many old-timers enjoy their *potica* with a slice of proscuitto, preferably homemade.

Antonucci's husband, Frank, who emigrated from Italy at age 14 to join his father working in the coal mines near Raton, finds that baking *potica* brings back a lot of memories of family members. "It was always in the family," he says. "When I taste *potica*, I think about them. It's part of the heritage, and it goes back a long time."

According to *Pots and Pans: A Slovenian-American Cookbook*, compiled and edited by Hermine Dicke and published by the Slovenian Women's Union

Opposite—Potica *bread baker Betty Antonucci of Raton loves the way baking this holiday treat reminds her of her mother.*

The dough must be rolled very thin and the rich filling spread evenly.

Rolling the potica is the most delicate part of the process. You don't want the dough to tear.

of America, the word "potica" means "something rolled in." While many kinds of filling may be used, either the plain walnut or the walnut and raisin or date remain the most popular. Other filling choices include chocolate, hazelnut, herbs (such as tarragon or chives) mixed with bread crumbs, pork cracklings, cottage cheese and poppyseed.

"*Potica* is as Slovenian as apple pie is American," writes Dicke. In the old days in Yugoslavia, it was made in quantity. The women used to mix it in washtubs, 100 loaves at a time. Then each woman would take loaves home to bake in her oven.

Potica, which freezes well, was traditionally baked the day before it was to be served. The round ceramic mold in which it was baked was known as a "toroidal," which means "with raised hole in the middle." Slovenian women would bless the dough with a sign of the cross before rolling it out "thin enough to read a newspaper by." To avoid air pockets, they pricked the dough with a knitting needle.

Potica is not easy to find; the search for it may become something of a quest. Two bakeries, one in Raton and one in Gallup, used to sell it at Christmastime. I now order my *poticas* from Gagliano's, an Italian specialty shop in Pueblo, Colorado, that has been baking them since 1928. I make the trek north over Thanksgiving weekend to pick them up. *Poticas* make great holiday gifts, and they freeze well. Several bakeries in Pueblo produce them. In fact, townspeople say, "If you have a tamale in one hand and a *potica* in the other, anyone can tell you are from Pueblo."

Baking *potica* is an elaborate and time-consuming process that requires patience and skill. One of New Mexico's champion *povitica* bakers, Luby Grenko of Gallup, says, "It's a lot of work, but I'm used to it. I go one, two, three, and the dough is all over the kitchen table. My husband made me a special board that covers the table, and I put a tablecloth on top of that. There's no rolling pin. I just use my hands. I just keep pulling it. I always have good luck. If you don't get your dough just right, with just enough and not too much flour, you're in trouble. If the dough starts breaking and getting holes in it, just forget about it and throw it away."

Grenko learned the art by watching her aunt. She started her baking in October every year and froze the bread, estimating that in her lifetime she baked "every bit of" 2,000 *poviticas*. Grenko recommends serving these savory treats with coffee, ice cream or Jell-O.

If you do not happen to have a loving Italian or Croatian aunt or grandmother to bake *potica* bread, you can create your own from the following recipe.

This story originally appeared in the Santa Fe New Mexican *in November 2004.*

RECIPES

Betty Antonucci's Potica Bread—a citrus-scented loaf that is very rich but not too sweet.
(Makes 3 loaves)

Yeast mixture:

> ½ cup warm milk
> 2 packages yeast
> 1 tablespoon sugar

Dissolve yeast in warm milk. Add sugar and let the mixture stand in a warm place until foamy, about 10 minutes.

Dough:

> 4 cups sifted flour
> 1 teaspoon salt
> ⅓ cup sugar (less that used for yeast)
> ¼ pound butter at room temperature
> 3 beaten egg yolks
> 1 cup sour cream at room temperature

Pour flour into a large bowl. Add salt, sugar, softened butter, beaten eggs and sour cream. Add the yeast mixture; mix well.

Knead until the dough is pliant, about 10 minutes. Divide into three parts. Place each part in a separate greased pan. Cover with waxed paper and cloth. Let rise in a warm place ½ hour.

(Recipe continues on page 24.)

Filling:

> 1½ pounds ground walnuts
> 1½ cups sweet cream
> 3 egg yolks
> ¼ pound sweet butter, melted
> 3 egg whites beaten stiff
> ⅓ cup honey
> 1 tablespoon orange rind
> 1 teaspoon vanilla
> 1 tablespoon brandy (peach)
> 1 tablespoon lemon rind
> 1½ cups sugar
> 1 lightly beaten egg white (for egg wash)

Scald the cream and pour it over chopped nuts. Add melted butter and let the mixture stand for 10 minutes. Add honey and sugar; mix well. Add lemon and orange rind, vanilla, brandy and slightly beaten egg yolks. Mix again.

Add 1 tablespoon sugar to egg whites and beat until stiff. Fold into nut mixture and set aside.

Roll out dough on a lightly floured cloth or tabletop to a ⅛-inch-thick oblong shape.

Spread nut mixture in a thin layer over the rolled dough, leaving an inch border all around. Roll up the dough like a jelly roll.

Tuck in the ends to seal as you roll. Prick occasionally with a fork to allow air to escape. Seal at the end.

Prick the top of the roll several times. Place roll in a greased pan or on a cookie sheet. Brush with egg white mixed with a little water.

Bake at 350 degrees F for ½ hour. Lower temperature to 325 degrees F. Bake for ½ hour. Let pie cool completely before slicing.

Note from Betty: "This dough is much easier to work with than the old-time recipe. I think it's because of the addition of sour cream, which makes for a dough much easier to roll out. And it's thinner, too." She has been baking *potica* every holiday season for at least 45 years, from the time she first began helping her mother.

For those who grew up in the coal mining towns where potica bread was served every Christmas and Easter, the holidays just aren't complete without it.

The 55-mph, two-lane road west of Socorro may at first appear barren and dusty, but for those who keep their eyes on the pie, there is no richer turf in New Mexico. To travel this "Pieway" is to find what is indisputably worthwhile in life—homemade pie. If you are a pie aficionado, this could be the trip of a lifetime. Get an early start and remember—this is no day for dieting.

Along this 102-mile stretch of U.S. 60 that unfurls across the broad Plains of San Agustín toward hazy, blue mountains and the Arizona border, home cooking is the only kind of sustenance you will find. In a refreshing change of pace, not a single fast-food establishment is in sight. Most likely, franchises stay away because there is not enough traffic to support them. But the lack of traffic and slower speed limit are reasons to take this road in the first place.

Instead, punctuating this quiet highway are mom-and-pop cafés diligently dishing out authentic fare to ranchers, truckers and tourists who meander through. A fractured history of New Mexico may be pieced together from the haunted ruins of the Kelly Mine, Magdalena's deserted stockyards and Charles Ilfeld's warehouse. The Very Large Array radio telescope with its 27 moveable giant dish antennas is neighbor to the 20th-century homesteading community of Pie Town, documented by Russell Lee's Depression-era photographs. The town straddling the Great Divide once was a stop for cowboys driving their cattle along the hoof highway from Springerville, Arizona, to the Magdalena railhead.

U.S. 60, established circa 1912, was the nation's first transcontinental road, often called the ocean-to-ocean highway. A hearty debate exists as to whether this stretch of roadway ever really was part of the original high-

Opposite—*Pie Town's reputation for serving the best pie along the road endures in the stalwart Pie-O-Neer Café, where you can choose among more than a half-dozen varieties.*

RECIPES

This is the piecrust recipe we use at home. It was given to us by my husband's mother, and it has never let us down.

Eloise Henry's Never Fail Piecrust (Makes 2 9-inch piecrusts)

> 2 cups flour
> 1 teaspoon salt
> ½ cup oil
> ¼ cup cold milk

Sift flour and salt together.

Pour milk and oil together, add to flour, and mix. Form into a ball and roll out between 2 sheets of wax paper.

Bake at 450 degrees F for 15 minutes.

Pie-O-Neer Café Piecrust (Makes 5 crusts)

> 5 cups flour
> ½ teaspoon baking powder
> 2 teaspoons salt
> 1 cup cold butter, cubed
> 1 cup lard
> 1 teaspoon vinegar (Apple cider is preferred.)
> 1 cup cold water (more/less)
> 1 egg

way. The answer is beyond the scope of our concern, which is, after all, pie.

Pie Town is one of the state's most unusual community names. Robert Julyan, author of *The Place Names of New Mexico*, cites the research of Kathryn McKee-Roberts, which relates the story of a gas station owner, Clyde Norman (some residents say it was Herman L. Norman), who began selling apple pies in the 1920s at Norman's Place. In 1924, Norman Craig bought out the owner and continued the pie-making enterprise with his wife and daughters. The citizens requested the name Pie Town for a post office in 1927. Local lore says when the inspector suggested a more conventional name, Craig said, "It'll either be named Pie Town, or you can take your PO and go to hell."

Fortunately, the name stuck and has inspired area chefs to continue the pie-baking tradition. Today's travelers can still go on a quest to sample the best homemade pies along U.S. 60. Because these are mom-and-pop establishments, however, hours and days of operation can change, so it's best to call ahead.

Starting in Magdalena, the first town west of Socorro, head for the Magdalena Café & Steakhouse at 109 S. Main St., where breakfast and lunch are served Monday through Saturday and dinner is available Thursday and Friday. Go for the fruit pie—peach is swell—over the chocolate, unless you prefer your pie super sweet. The café occupies the former Masonic Lodge.

Back on the corner of U.S. 60 and N. Main, in the old bank building that refuses to burn down, is Evett's Café & Fountain, a mother lode of nostalgia, where you can find a more savory treat, the Frito Pie. Yes, the Frito Pie counts as a pie. Evett's version, smothered in homemade red or green chile, compares favorably with those served in the school gymnasiums of northern New Mexico. You can savor your bowl of chile-saturated chips with a float, malt or shake at the original counter with fountain. Evett's is open daily.

Keep moving. Keep heading west. When you step into the Eagle Guest Ranch in Datil, at the junction of U.S. 60 and N.M. 12, you have entered the Wild West of Catron County. The opinions of outsiders, particularly environmentalists and wolf-lovers, are definitely not appreciated here, so check yours at the door. The Eagle Guest Ranch has been in the same family since 1920, when it started as a store and post office. Later, the owners added gas pumps. Hunters, cowboys and good ol' boys frequent this establishment. This burger haven/steakhouse is known for its blazing hot Mexican food generally served on Fridays, and its apple pie satisfies the urge for homemade pie when nothing else will do.

Sift together flour, salt and baking powder into a large bowl.

Using either a pastry cutter or a food processor cut in butter and lard, without overworking the mixture. If using a processor, just a few pulses should do.

Crack an egg into a measuring cup. Add vinegar and beat slightly with a fork. Add cold water to measure just over 1 cup.

Slowly add the liquid mixture to the dry mixture, making sure to bring up the dry mix from the bottom of the bowl. After using all the liquid, the dough should start holding together. If it looks a bit dry, just add a little more water.

Spread a small amount of flour on your work surface. Gently make 5 patties. Wrap the dough in Saran Wrap and chill for at least an hour.

For a 2-crust pie, roll out 2 patties on a floured surface. Place one in a pie pan and keep the other covered until ready to use. The less you touch the dough, the flakier the crust will be.

Wrap unused dough in Saran Wrap and aluminum foil and freeze.

Kathy Knapp's New Mexico Apple Pie (Serves 8)

5–6 large or 6–8 medium-sized apples (½ Granny Smith's and ½ any other kind of apples except Delicious)

½ cup sugar (more or less to taste)

Cinnamon to taste

1 tablespoon cornstarch or any thickener you prefer

1 cup roasted and chopped green chiles, hot as you like. If using canned, drain well.

1 cup unsalted piñon nuts, roasted

Pats of butter

1 lightly beaten egg white (for egg wash)

Slice apples thin to medium. Mix sugar, cinnamon and cornstarch in a bowl and combine with apples. Stir in green chiles and piñon nuts. Mound into the pie shell. Dot with butter. Put top crust on, sealing the edges and brushing the top with egg wash.

Decorate the top with leftover crust scraps shaped like chiles. Using a knife, slice small steam vents in the top crust and bake in a hot oven (425–450 degrees F) for 15–20 minutes. Then turn the oven down to 350 degrees F and finish baking for another 40–45 minutes or until the pie is golden brown and bubbling.

Some say the Eagle Guest Ranch serves better pie, at a better price, than neighboring Pie Town establishments. You be the judge.

Still, Pie Town is the destination. The two operating Pie Town establishments, Daily Pie and the Pie-O-Neer Café, continue the tradition that began in the 1920s. Kathy Knapp, proprietor of the Pie-O-Neer for the past dozen years, understands the pie mystique.

"Homemade pie is part of the journey. It evokes a good feeling. It's reminiscent of mom and grandma in the kitchen, with family gathered around. It's the last vestige of home. There's such an appreciation for something made by hand with love."

Knapp opened the café in 1995 with her mother, when, during a vacation, they found this 1940s-era building vacant. "If you buy it," her mother said, "I'll bake 'em and they'll come." Knapp's mother and grandmother ran a café in Rochelle, Illinois, so with their experience and the family's enthusiasm, they gave it a go.

Among Knapp's most popular pies are her sour cherry pie; coconut cream pie from her grandmother's recipe, which won a *Sunset Magazine* recipe contest; and her New Mexico green chile apple piñon pie, which inspired a short film titled *A Piece of Pie*.

The café is open Friday through Monday. If she sells

out, Knapp closes early. The café sells pies by the slice, and you may order a whole pie in advance.

I am also a fan of the Daily Pie Café. Crusts are tender, and fillings achieve the right balance of tartness and sweet fruitiness. Daily Pie displays a "pie chart," which on any given day will feature cherry, peach, strawberry-rhubarb (the best seller), New Mexico apple and the special "Primo," a blackberry-blueberry combo. Despite its name, the café is not open daily. It is closed on Sunday and Monday. Daily Pie also serves burgers and fries, soups, a barbecue pulled-pork basket and all-around tasty lunches.

Last stop on the tour is the Largo Café in Quemado. Pies here are beautiful, with perfect toasty-brown crusts. The fillings, however, are a bit lacking in texture, more on the preserve side than I like. The sign out front says, "We think we have New Mexico's best green chile cheeseburger," a tossed gauntlet if there ever was one. You may need some protein to balance the sugar at this point, so perhaps you will want to put that claim to the test.

The annual Pie Town Pie Festival generally occurs the second Saturday of September. It's best to arrive early. If you intend to enter the pie contest, bring two identical pies, one for the judges and one for tasting.

When pears are in season, Kathy Knapp is inspired to make her French Pear with Ginger Pie. (Serves 8)

> 5 large Bartlett pears
> 3 tablespoons frozen orange juice concentrate (or marmalade)
> ½ teaspoon grated lemon zest
> 1 tablespoon fresh grated ginger
> ¾ cup flour
> ½ cup sugar
> ⅛ teaspoon salt
> 1 teaspoon cinnamon
> ½ teaspoon ground ginger
> ⅓ cup butter

Peel, core and slice pears into a bowl. Add orange juice or marmalade, zest and fresh ginger. Arrange these ingredients in an unbaked pie shell.

In a separate bowl, mix all remaining ingredients, cutting the butter in last to make a crumbly topping. Spread the topping over the pears evenly, patting gently.

Bake at 400 degrees F for 40–45 minutes. Excellent with fresh whipped cream and strawberries!

Right—*Michele Wegner shows off Pie Town's Daily Pie Café's signature creation, the "Primo," a juicy, sweet-tart, blackberry-blueberry and lattice-crusted wonder.*

Opposite—*Pie Town's Daily Pie Café serves breakfast and lunch in addition to pie. While you just might want to eat dessert first, choosing what kind of pie to have could be your biggest challenge of the day.*

More than 30,000 hearty souls make the annual pilgrimage to Chimayó on Good Friday, many walking along the highways and back roads of northern New Mexico for days. Throughout the year, it's estimated that 300,000 others visit this "Lourdes of America," prayerfully seeking the curative powers of the "holy dirt" at El Santuario (The Shrine) de Chimayó. Discarded crutches and notes of thanks for answered prayers fill the little prayer room left of the altar. A statue of Santo Niño de Atocha, considered a manifestation of the Holy Child, has a place of prominence. Santo Niño, beloved by northern New Mexico Catholics, is said to wear out his shoes as he goes about the village at night, performing good deeds for the faithful. Shafts of filtered light illuminate pilgrims kneeling before the glass-encased figure. Tiny replacement shoes are left here for him, and many more are lined up in the chapel dedicated to him across the road.

But another breed of pilgrim journeys faithfully to Chimayó. This tribe comes seeking a different, but, they would say, related form of revelation that sparks the heart by means of the senses. The holy ground of Chimayó produces a chile that is as actively sought as were the rare spices of old, with reverence, dedication and intense passion. There is no substitute for Chimayó chile—and the faithful insist there is none better. Watered by the acequia that runs through the village, the chile's thin-skinned, comparatively small crimson pods contain a sweet-hot fire that warms the tongue, the belly and the soul. The elongated heart-shaped pod, recognizable by the curl atop its stem—can take the chill off a cold winter's evening or bring a cooling sweat to the brow on a sweltering summer afternoon. Along with small canisters of holy dirt found in El Santuario, the seekers of true chile

Opposite—*Patty Albritton and Angel Reyes tend fields of flowers, chile and corn in Chimayó with a plow drawn by El Macho, their mule.*

Art and brilliant crimson chile ristras line the narrow roadway that leads to El Santuario de Chimayó, a place that many seek out because of their belief in the curative "holy dirt."

flavor bring home sacks of dried pods and bags of fine-textured, crimson Chimayó chile.

Unlike chile varieties developed at the New Mexico State University Chile Institute that are grown commercially in Hatch, the Mesilla Valley and along the Río Grande, Chimayó chile is a "landrace" plant, descended from native seed. The heirloom chile has been grown by local folks for generations, passed down through the families and traded with neighbors.

The Chimayó Chile Project was established in 2003 to revive the local native strain. Seeds for the chile are now available to local growers at the town feed store.

As most chile grown here is consumed here, too, the best way to ensure your purchase of genuine Chimayó chile is to make your own pilgrimage to Chimayó. There, in September and October, you can stroll up the path leading to El Santuario. The walkway is wide enough for pilgrims walking side by side or a burro carrying a load of wood. Curtains of scarlet ristras drape the autumn sunlight and emit a pure aroma that nourishes both body and soul.

There are several accounts regarding a miracle that led to the building of El Santuario. The most prevalent relates to Bernardo Abeyta in about

1810. It is said that the *hermano* (Penitente brother) was performing Good Friday rituals when he saw a light emanating from a distant hill. He dug at the spot and found a crucifix of Our Lord of Esquipulas, a Guatemalan religious figure. The crucifix was brought to the nearby Santa Cruz mission, yet, miraculously, it reappeared in the spot where Abeyta originally found it. The mysterious event happened three times. Finally, circa 1816, Abeyta built El Santuario to honor the vision. The well of holy dirt is located today where Abeyta saw his vision, and the crucifix rests behind the altar.

The name "Chimayó" is derived from a Tewa word, *tsi mayoh*, meaning "hill of the east." And the *posito*, or well of holy dirt, is said to be located on the spot of hot springs—now dried up—where indigenous people made pilgrimages. No wonder that even the skeptics have reported feelings of deep spiritual connection here, often to their own surprise.

Chimayó may be approached from many directions. It is located 40 miles south of Taos, 24 miles northeast of Santa Fe and 10 miles from Española up N.M. 76. A journey down from Taos can take you along the winding High Road, past the remote villages of Truchas, Vadito and Peñasco. Very little has changed since the Spanish settled here in the 18th and 19th centuries. Descendants of original land-grant families still dwell here, practicing the old ways. Many live off the land—cutting wood, growing and preserving fruits and vegetables, bartering, and making what they need with their own hands.

While the shops on Santuario Lane sell delicious sun-dried Chimayó chile as a kitchen ingredient, you can satisfy your appetite for local cuisine at nearby eateries. Leona's, located directly to the left of El Santuario, is a mod-

Devotees of Chimayó chile claim you will never find chile as pure, delicious and flavorful as the chile grown in Chimayó. The chile plants are cultivated from ancient seeds and watered by the village acequias.

It is a rare and precious sight to find corn drying in the sun. *Chicos*, the regional Spanish word for the preserved corn, is frequently combined in cooking with beans to make a perfect protein.

est, reliable and friendly hole-in-the-wall that serves delicious, authentic chile. Leona is famous for her fresh, handmade tortillas. A bit more upscale, and just down the lane and to the right, is Rancho de Chimayó, a beautiful, classic northern New Mexico restaurant that has long been in the Jaramillo family. The sopaipillas with honey are divine, and there's nothing better than a margarita by the fireplace in winter.

Patty Albritton, a Chimayó native, farms her grandmother's 6 acres on the Cañada Ancha acequia with the help of her partner, Angel Reyes, her grandson Kaeden Albritton, and a mule named El Macho. They grow native Chimayó chile, corn to be preserved as *chicos*, sweet peas and onions. Colorful flowers and dried corn are used in the arrangements and decorations they make by hand and sell at farmers markets in Los Alamos and Taos. They believe the old-fashioned plow drawn by El Macho, their mule, controls soil erosion and weeds better than a tractor.

RECIPES

Here are two of Patty Albritton's recipes using Chimayó chile from her forthcoming cookbook, *Chile New Mexico Style*.

Chile Estillo Nuevo Mexico (Chicken with Lemongrass and Chile in Caramel Sauce)
(Serves 4)

> 3 pounds chicken
> 1 large onion
> 1 teaspoon ground Chimayó chile
> 1 tablespoon granulated sugar
> 1 cup water
> 4 cloves garlic
> 3 tablespoons vegetable oil
> 2 tablespoons minced lemongrass (available at Asian markets)
> 4 tablespoons fish sauce (available at Asian markets)
> 1 tablespoon caramel sauce

Rinse the chicken and dry well. Cut it into small pieces.

Peel garlic and slice finely. Slice onion.

Heat oil in a large frying pan over medium heat. Add a pinch of salt, garlic and onion. Fry over medium heat until onion becomes translucent. Add lemongrass and chile.

Fry 1 to 2 minutes until fragrant. Add the chicken and cook until lightly browned.

Add fish sauce, sugar and caramel sauce. Mix well.

Add 1 cup water and cook 45 minutes or until the chicken is tender. Stir occasionally and add more water if necessary. Taste and correct for spices. Serve over rice.

Caramel Sauce

Mix ½ cup sugar with 4 tablespoons of water in a heavy saucepan. Bring to a boil over medium heat and let the mixture cook until it changes color. Turn the heat down to low, and heat until brown.

Add ½ cup water to the mixture. Stir until sugar is dissolved. Remove from heat and store in a jar in the refrigerator.

Chile Nightmare
(Serves 4)

    1 cup cooked, dried pinto beans
    2 tablespoons lard
    1 tablespoon bacon drippings
    1 chopped onion
    12 ounces pork sausage
    1 pound ground beef
    4 garlic cloves
    1 ground cinnamon stick
    1 teaspoon fresh ground black pepper
    1 teaspoon ground nutmeg
    2 teaspoons dried oregano
    4 teaspoons sesame seeds
    1 cup blanched almonds, skins removed
    8 dried red chiles
    ½ cup chile caribe (coarse ground chile)
    1 can tomato paste (6 ounces)
    2 tablespoons vinegar
    3 teaspoons lemon juice

Drain beans, reserving cooking liquid.

Melt the lard in a heavy skillet over medium heat. Add beans and lightly fry them in the lard. Set aside.

Melt bacon drippings in a large, heavy pot over medium heat. Add onion and cook until translucent.

Combine sausage and beef with all spices up through the oregano. Add this meat-and-spice mixture to the pot with the onion. Break up any lumps with a fork and cook, stirring occasionally, until the meat is very well browned. Drain.

Add water only if necessary to maintain the consistency of a chunky soup. Stir in all remaining ingredients. Bring to a boil, lower the heat and cook.

Taste when curiosity becomes unbearable and courage is strong. Adjust seasonings.

Serve with corn chips, shredded cheese, sour cream, guacamole, grated onion and more beans. Great for football watching on wintry Sunday afternoons.

The Best Red Chile Enchiladas
(Serves 4)

- 1 dozen corn tortillas
- 1½ pounds ground round
- 1 large yellow onion, chopped
- 4 cloves garlic, minced
- 1 medium brick yellow Longhorn Colby cheese, grated
- 8–10 medium to large red chile pods
- Canola oil sufficient for frying

Brown the ground round over medium heat in a heavy skillet.

As the meat is browning, toast chile pods lightly in a cast-iron pan or the oven for about 10 minutes or until fragrant. Seed and stem the pods.

Cover pods with boiling water until softened, about 10 minutes. Place pods in a blender about ¾ full. Add 1 cup cold water and blend about 5 minutes.

Mince garlic and sauté. Add blended chile and ½ teaspoon salt and bring the mixture to a boil. Lower heat, cover and simmer about 15 minutes.

Heat each tortilla in a medium-hot frying pan using a thin layer of canola oil.

In a well-greased 9×13 pan, layer heated tortillas, cheese, drained beef and onion and top with a layer of red chile. Do this until all ingredients are used. Sprinkle the top with grated cheese.

Bake until bubbly at 325 degrees F for about 20 minutes.

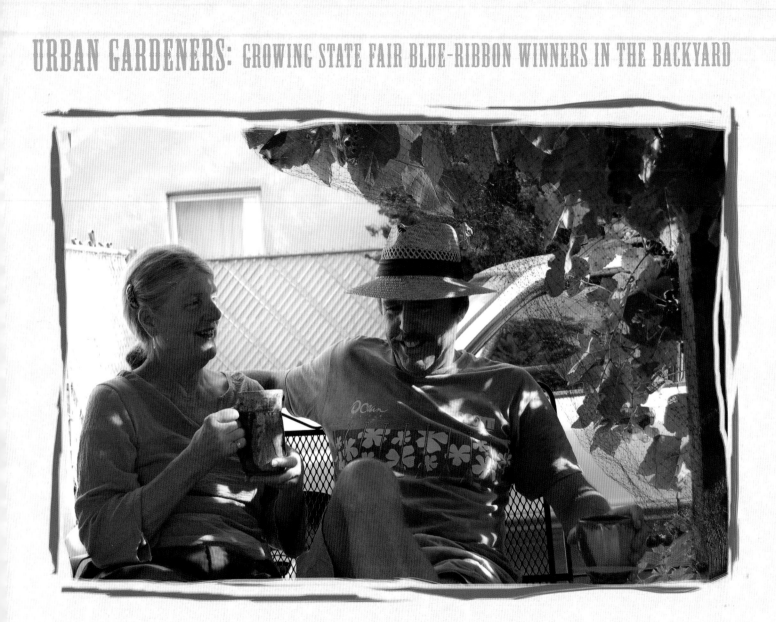

L ong before turning the front lawn into a turnip patch became fashionable, David Kammer and Jeanne Whitehouse were growing their own food in their urban Albuquerque neighborhood on a side street between two heavily trafficked university-area boulevards. Entering their garden, which bursts with healthy productivity in the middle of the city, is as magical as finding a fairy-tale cottage in the midst of a thick forest.

The couple's flexible occupations have granted them the time to commit to their shared passion. Whitehouse is a teacher and author of children's literature (published under the name Jeanne Whitehouse Peterson); Kammer is a popular historian, consultant and speaker. Now that they are semi-retired, their urban garden has become the flourishing centerpiece of their lives. The growing season rules their year. They work in the garden several hours every morning and do not travel between April and September. They have a bit of down time during November and December, but their gardening season begins anew when the seed catalogs arrive in January.

Kammer and Whitehouse have entered their urban produce in the New Mexico State Fair for 25 years. They usually compete in 15 to 20 different contests, but their chile collection remains their pride and joy. They have won dozens of blue ribbons for their brilliantly colored and meticulous arrangements of chile peppers. Each variety they grow and show is a source of button-bursting pride.

The twosome strives to keep the care and feeding of the garden as sustainable as possible. They collect water in 150-gallon rain barrels, and in winter they gather leaves up and down the street for compost and mulch. To conserve water they employ drip and soaker systems for irrigating their

Above—*David Kammer is proud of his simple and effective rain-collection system. His urban gardening success comes from persistence, patience and never wasting a drop of water.*

Opposite—*Jeanne Whitehouse and David Kammer enjoy a coffee break under their front porch grapevine.*

Jeanne Whitehouse is especially fond of her pink zinnias, which grow prolifically in her front yard along with her other plants.

1,800-square-foot garden. When they moved into their 1,100-square-foot WWII stucco home in 1987, they had only a lone juniper in their yard.

Today after years of careful cultivation they have 10 fruit trees, including apple, peach, plum, pear, cherry and fig. They are especially enchanted with their rare heirloom apples, in particular, the 17th-century apple called New Towne Pippin. Nine grapevines and a raspberry patch also flourish in their yard. The beauty and abundance of their harvest is astounding.

From their front porch, they have the pleasure of viewing a yard they have cultivated in squash, chiles and tomatoes mixed in a profusion of pink zinnias, crimson amaranth and four o'clocks.

"We have all the tomatoes, peppers, beans, squash and cukes we can eat," says Kammer. "We never buy tomatoes." Their drying, canning and freezing keeps them well supplied most of the year, plus there is a "feeling of freshness" about their food that can't be bought in a grocery store.

The couple's backgrounds do carry hints of their dedication to bringing forth fruit from the earth. Kammer grew up in New Jersey, which is known as "The Garden State." My own memories of New Jersey summers include luscious blueberries, tomatoes, corn and melons bought at farmers markets and roadside stands. His mother's family farmed in Pennsylvania's Susquehanna Valley.

Kammer grew up with a big backyard garden and remembers helping transform the property into a fertile space. Creating a productive garden in northeast Albuquerque came naturally. Earning a doctorate and becoming a working historian did not diminish the urge to plant and grow.

Whitehouse, too, had agriculture in her blood, through the connec-

RECIPES

The Kammer-Whitehouse family shares two of their favorite recipes. Both are made with fresh herbs and vegetables from their urban garden.

Basil Vinaigrette

Says Whitehouse: "The grandchildren call this 'basil sauce' and love to spread or drizzle it on nine-grain bread with cheese. We use it in place of mayonnaise or mustard, on just about anything. And 1 or 2 tablespoons can easily be combined with olive oil to make a dressing for pasta or vegetable salads. It freezes well."

½ cup chopped onion
1 garlic clove, chopped
½ teaspoon yellow mustard seeds
¼ teaspoon salt or to taste
½ cup olive oil or olive/canola mix
2 cups fresh sweet basil leaves, broken into bits
¼ cup rice vinegar
½ teaspoon oregano or to taste

Combine all ingredients in a blender. Blend until well mixed. Serve.

Top—*The couple inspect and work in their garden every morning.*

Above—*The reward is a bountiful harvest. Some of their yield will be dried, and some will be consumed fresh.*

Jeanne Whitehouse and David Kammer have taken home many prizes from the New Mexico State Fair. This colorful, artistic chile basket added another blue ribbon to their collection.

tion to her ranching family in Lake County, Oregon. "Women were always talking about preparing displays for the fair," she recalls.

The pair has learned by doing and from the wisdom of their circle of gardening friends. Their garden has no straight lines. They have learned to plant closely and in circles to encourage volunteer plants. They try to grow foods not available in stores, and they favor heirloom produce. And, yes, they are organic growers, using hand picking, timed planting, and soap and water to get rid of pests. They have concocted their own mixture of soap, garlic and chile pepper to stave off undesirable bugs.

Each bean plant and every squash blossom is noticed, acknowledged and treated with tender respect. The duo is always willing to be surprised.

Events have caught up with Kammer and Whitehouse. First Lady Michelle Obama has planted a vegetable garden on the South Lawn of the White House. Author Michael Pollan has made the best-seller list with books advocating locally grown food. Well-watered lawns have become just about passé in the Southwest.

Now the couple's garden is as much a model for the future as it remains a tie to their pasts. They are lifestyle pioneers; what has long made sense to them has begun to make sense for the larger culture.

Growing fruits and vegetables in the desert Southwest isn't always easy.

"Living with hail, wind and rains, and living close to the airport, make this a special challenge," says Kammer, who also tends grapes at their rental property down the street. All their lives together they have composted and built fertile soil in this gravelly section of the East Mesa at the base of the Sandías, nourishing roots despite the hard caliche soil underneath. "Gardening strips you of hubris," he adds.

Living in harmony with the land in an urban environment, however, has its rewards. Raising children and grandchildren, creating a home, living within the cycles of the year even in the middle of a sprawling high-desert cityscape, planting, tending, harvesting, and preserving—they're all part of building a rich life together.

Tomato Confit

2–4 cups cherry tomatoes or chopped
   Roma tomatoes
5–8 cloves garlic, minced
3 sprigs fresh rosemary twigs, stripped of
   leaves and minced
Sprinkle sea salt
¼ to ½ teaspoon ground cayenne pepper
   (optional)
2-3 tablespoons olive oil

Preheat oven to 375 degrees F. Spray glass baking dish with nonstick spray.

Layer in tomatoes. Cover with garlic, salt and remaining ingredients.

Bake for ½ hour–45 minutes. Stir occasionally. Do not let tomatoes get too browned. Remove, let cool in pan, and serve with crackers and cheese.

Top, left—*Jeanne Whitehouse shows off the large squash that thrives among the sunflowers.*

Below, left—*David Kammer checks his heirloom apples, which are almost ripe enough to pick.*

Opposite—*Jeanne Whitehouse admires the prolific growth in her Albuquerque garden.*

L atkes. Like the matzoh ball, kugel, gefilte fish and challah, the latke is so much more than an assemblage of its ingredients. This little potato pancake is rarely referred to in the singular, however. When latkes are great, they must be served in abundance, sizzling hot from the oil. Preparing, reveling in the aroma of, and finally, tasting the perfect latke—precisely salted and peppered, subtly scented with onion—is a centuries-old Jewish tradition.

This experience is a centerpiece in the celebration of Chanukah, the Festival of Lights. The eight-day holiday commemorates the miracle of the oil, when the Temple in Jerusalem was rededicated after the Jewish people successfully revolted against assimilation and religious oppression in the second century B.C. There was only enough oil to light the eternal flame in the Temple for one day, yet it miraculously burned for eight days.

The perfect latke, that delectable pancake usually prepared only once a year, at Chanukah, is a miracle in itself. This treat may seem simple to make, but its creation requires a practiced and patient chef. Latkes generally come in two kinds: thin and crispy, scarcely seconds from being burnt, or gooey, thick and bluish. Like many of life's simple pleasures, superb latkes are not easy to achieve, and from them much is expected.

During the days of Chanukah, Jews light the menorah, the nine-branched candelabrum that gains a candle a night for a week, increasing the light at the darkest time of the year. They also spin the dreidle, playing a children's game with a top, and give gifts and gold-wrapped chocolate coins called Chanukah gelt. But above all, the celebration of Chanukah requires a feast of latkes.

Opposite—*When fried crispy and golden brown, the humble potato pancake becomes a delectable treat. Latkes have made a long, slow migration from Germany and Eastern Europe to the banks of the Río Grande. Served with sour cream and applesauce, they are the one essential Chanukah dish.*

New Mexico artist Anita Rodriguez, who divides her time between Taos and Mexico, includes references to the legacy of the Crypto-Jews in this painting. The Sabbath candles and challah, a traditional Jewish bread, are seen beneath the image of Our Lady of Guadalupe. Using florescent colors and Day of the Dead imagery, she depicts the figures leading colorful lives.

Painting from the author's collection.

Diners eat their fill, and more, at this special meal of latkes, accompanied by generous bowls of sour cream and applesauce. Both diets and cholesterol concerns are tossed out with the potato peels. Latke making is often a team sport, with family and guests participating in the peeling and grating of potatoes and onions and sharing fry duty at the stove. The "latke party" is a re-creation, knowingly or unconsciously, of the gathering of the tribe—the family—on a cold, dark, winter's night.

The feast is for remembrance's sake. The latke comes to the table laden with centuries of tradition, childhood memories of festive occasions and the powerful yearning to reconnect to one's origins.

A lot to ask of a potato pancake, you say? But Jews here in the Southwest—no longer in Odessa or Minsk or Warsaw or even Baltimore or Great Neck or East Orange—are far from their origins. They left home so long ago and so far behind that bittersweet memories are triggered vividly by the scent of a potato pancake sizzling in a hot iron skillet. The taste of that little latke evokes memories of a loving *bubbe* (grandmother) or busy mother preparing the treat and of the family gathering together in the warmth of the candles. When that forkful of pancake is dipped into applesauce and brought to the lips, the hope of remembering roots, no matter how distant, is renewed.

Identity can indeed be a touchy issue for those who have left home. Even now, it is not unusual for a Jewish person living in New Mexico to be asked by an East Coast relative, "So, are there any Jews out there?"

Yes, Aunt Sadie, there are Jews on the Río Grande. In the thousands. And synagogues and rabbis and Chanukah. And a Jewish legacy, too.

Some of the original settlers of this land fled Spain to avoid religious persecution during the time of the Spanish Inquisition. They made their way up El Camino Real along the Río Grande. The details of their private spiritual lives here remain mysterious. They left neither written records nor artifacts. Very few of their customs have lived on in the memories of their descendants in isolated villages. Clues, however, are found on headstone carvings in remote cemeteries. In recent years more has been discovered about these Crypto-Jews, the hidden ones who disguised themselves within another faith to survive persecution. It is known that here, on the other side of the world, they publicly hid their religious identities and, at the same time, honored their origins in private. Artists, poets, historians and dreamers now provide the link to their presence. Diana Bryer and Anita Rodriguez are two artists who have incorporated references to the Crypto-Jews in their work.

Later, in the mid-19th century, another wave of Jewish immigrants, the German-Jewish pioneers, made their way here as merchants, traders and ranchers who created homes from Santa Fe to Tucumcari. They learned Spanish and Native languages, traded, helped build communities, found-

RECIPES

The Best Latkes Ever (Serves 2-3)

To create the best latkes, you cannot take shortcuts, and you cannot substitute ingredients.

If you want the tastiest, crispiest, most delightful latkes you, your family, and your guests have ever put in their mouths, you must follow these directions exactly. You cannot grate the potatoes in a food processor. They must be grated by hand. You cannot substitute cracker crumbs; rather, you must go on a quest for matzoh meal. Many recipes invite experimentation or the addition of the personal touch, but this one does not. Latkes may take a little longer and require a little more care, but the results are worth your investment of time. I have researched latkes thoroughly, over many years, and have constructed this recipe by borrowing from the best.

My recipe begins on the next page.

ed schools, built synagogues, and participated in local and state politics. Here they found the freedom to marry, own property, do business, pray and live openly—all that was denied them in Europe. Descendants of these 19th-century pioneers still reside in New Mexico. And it is quite likely they, and others who celebrate Chanukah in the Southwest, enjoy latkes at their festivities.

Yet the latkes served to holiday revelers may not live up to the perfectly tasty cakes of memory, even in the hands of cooks of good reputation. Guests might confront greasy, half-raw, half-burnt latkes on their plates. Or, instead of beautiful, brown little cakes, the latkes may turn out doughy and too blue. To avoid these pitfalls, follow the accompanying tried-and-true recipe.

4 very crisp russet potatoes (Save the Yukon
　　golds and Peruvian blues for another
　　time.)
1 egg
1 onion
¼ cup matzoh meal
Salt and pepper to taste
Canola oil sufficient for frying
Sour cream
Applesauce

Peel the potatoes. Soak each potato in a bowl
of cold water as you peel the next. Grate potatoes by hand. Cover the bowl with plastic wrap
and refrigerate for 15 minutes. Remove and
squeeze out the liquid that has accumulated.

Grate the onion by hand. Add it to the potato
mixture, along with matzoh meal.

Separate the egg. Beat the yolk. Add it to the
mixture.

Beat the egg white by hand with a manual
eggbeater until it peaks, like meringue. Fold in
the egg white gently.

Add enough oil to the pan—cast iron is best—
until it is covered by at least ½ inch of oil. Heat
until the oil is very hot. Fling in a drop of potato
batter to see if it sizzles before beginning.

On a medium flame, add to the hot oil a
large tablespoon of potato mixture for each
latke. Flatten with the back of a spoon or a
spatula.

Fry until crispy brown all over; the edges
should be just shy of burnt. Turn once. When
richly browned on both sides, drain each
latke on a paper towel. Keep them warm in
a low oven, around 250 degrees F.

Latkes are traditionally served with sour
cream and applesauce. They may accom-
pany a roast brisket.

For those with dietary concerns, a not-bad
latke can be made using nonstick spray
instead of oil and egg substitute instead of
eggs. These are not as delicious as the real
thing, but they are satisfying. Fat-free sour
cream and sugar-free applesauce are other
good options.

"When we'd go out we got so hungry that when we'd get back to camp at night we were like bears. We just couldn't wait hardly until the meal was ready and we'd gather around the fire the cook had and he got mad and swore around quite a bit... We'd gather round and tell how saddle sore we were and how many stickers we'd got in us and how uncomfortable we were and how we didn't sleep at night and I know the minute we touched the bed we were all sound asleep and never woke up till morning but we had to complain you know, and those boys were tenderfeet."—**Marietta Wetherill, describing the archaeological expedition into Grand Gulch, Utah, with her husband, explorer Richard Wetherill, and Harvard students**

The cast-iron Dutch oven is possibly the most durable, ample and forgiving cooking utensil ever created. From the time the first cast-iron vessel left the blacksmith's forge, humanity has relied on this sturdy pot with a tight-fitting lid to cook stews, soups and roasts. It's even used to bake biscuits and cobblers. It has not disappointed us yet. The sight of a Dutch oven on the fire is a guarantee of a meal that is hot, tasty and plentiful, more than sufficient to satisfy all the hungry folks gathered around the fire. It satisfies our primal needs not only for food but also for hearth and warmth, which aside from pure practicality might explain its endurance over centuries.

The Dutch oven has a special place in the history of New Mexico cookery. An essential for pioneers who traversed the Santa Fe Trail, homesteaders, miners and cowboys, it symbolizes our Southwestern roots. As a metaphor, it is steady, simple, strong and practical—much like the folks who

A shovelful of ashes on the lid creates a magnificent Dutch oven, turning cobbler crust into a mouth-watering golden-brown.

relied on it to feed themselves and their families out on the trail and later, on the range. The heavy, indestructible kettle was the centerpiece of the chuck wagon—that skillfully outfitted traveling kitchen that accompanied travelers on the westward journey across the arduous trails of North America. So versatile, it could bake, fry, roast and boil and eliminated the need for too many pots. It was the portable Crock-Pot of its day.

The chuck wagon was crammed with shelves of staples, such as beans, coffee, salt, sugar, canned fruit and flour. Add to this whatever was hunted, butchered, caught or foraged, and the cook prepared biscuits and gravy, cobblers, fried chicken, beefsteaks, roasts, bacon, eggs, fried fish and whatever else might be procured along the way.

Stories abound about the origin of the Dutch oven's name, which is to say that nobody really knows where it came from. Some say the Dutch first commercially made the pots, subsequently popularized by an Englishman. Others maintain the Pilgrims brought them to America. Perhaps they were called "Dutch" because Dutch or German peddlers sold them, or because they were first used by the Pennsylvania Dutch.

Early companies, such as Lodge, established in 1896 in Tennessee, manufactured skillets and pots of varying sizes, numbered by width. The camp oven has legs and a lipped lid, for coals. Even today, with all the modern cookware created, nothing has come along to beat cast iron's capability to hold heat and cook as thoroughly.

Another great feature about the Dutch oven is that it cleans up easily. Food does not stick to a well-seasoned Dutch oven, a particularly endearing characteristic to those who lacked running water. It is one of those items that improves with age and use. The more you use it, the better the seasoning. My best-seasoned skillet, onyx black and almost crusty, has been in my husband's family more than a century. It still makes the crispiest bacon and the best fried eggs, and I use it almost every day. In fact, I own cast-iron skillets small enough to fry a single egg and large enough to fry two chickens, so cast iron is still my preferred way of cooking. At last count, I had four good-sized Dutch ovens in my kitchen cabinet. I happen to think cast iron just cooks better than anything else. Once you have fixed flapjacks on a good, hot, well-seasoned cast-iron griddle, there is no going back to any other kind. I use mine so often—to warm tortillas or make grilled-cheese-and-green-chile sandwiches— that it stays on top of the stove.

And should you find a rusty Dutch oven, as I did, in a secondhand store in Clayton, snap it up. With some scrubbing and a thin coating of solid shortening—Crisco or lard—followed by a slow bake for a couple of hours at low heat, around 250 degrees F, you'll have yourself a good-as-new pot that will last a lifetime. When cleaning it, simply wipe it out with a paper towel, or if necessary, rinse with hot water, and dry over a low flame on the stove. It's important to dry it completely. Occasionally, it may need re-seasoning. The seasoning is the patina

There's no doubt that the most delectable sourdough biscuits are cooked in a Dutch oven.

on a Dutch oven, a small effort to make for a vessel that serves so well and faithfully.

The popularity of Dutch-oven cooking, as a link to the Old West, has grown in recent decades. In New Mexico, Dutch-oven cooking is celebrated in September at Solanofest, an annual cook-off in northeast New Mexico near Roy, and in October at Lincoln Cowboy Days in Ruidoso, to name just two places to admire the craft. The public can enter the cook-off competition, or at least sample the results of old-fashioned, cast-iron cookery.

But in some parts of New Mexico, such as the Shafer Gallacher Ranch in the Lincoln County *malpais* (badlands), the original, practical use of the Dutch oven has never died out. Jane Shafer continues to feed cowboys on the open range whenever they neighbor up for branding or moving cattle. She still serves from her Dutch ovens, inherited from her father. "My dad cooked in sheep camp, and he knew fire. He taught me, and I watched. I can make a fire anywhere," she says. "The fire is the main thing. You have to have your fire close." Instead of digging a trench, Shafer builds her fire directly on the ground. Then she places over the fire an iron grill her husband, Bobby Shafer, made with 6-inch pieces of pipe on the corners. She encloses her fire with weatherbeaten pieces of tin. "I use cedar, because that's what we have, but oak is excellent. Oak makes good coals. I like to cook with aspen—no smoke, no ashes."

"Dutch-oven cooks come down through each generation," she says. "Father taught Mother, then Mother taught me. When you bake in a Dutch oven, you need a lot of coals. You shovel out coals, put the lid on—it has to fit real tight—and shovel those coals on top of the lid. Now I'm the cook."

Immense pots of beans, *arroz con pollo*, biscuits and coffee, what Shafer calls the "Spanish meal," are served to hungry hardworking cowboys midday. Around mid-morning, she loads her pickup with basic ingredients and utensils, sets up near the cowboys' work area, gathers wood and starts the fire. As the fire dies down and coals form, she reads the heat for the proper time to begin her cooking. She instinctively knows how to turn her Dutch oven into a regular oven for baking peach or cherry cobbler by piling hot coals on the lid.

"You can cook anything in a Dutch oven," Shafer maintains. She handles six enormous pots with ease, occasionally raising a lid with her "goncho," the running branding iron traditionally used to hoist the heavy iron lids. "Nothing cooks better or keeps food hot longer," she says. Her rule of thumb for feeding a crowd is: use 6 pounds of meat—venison, beef, pork or mutton—to feed 24 people.

Above—*The well-equipped chuck wagon is a traveling kitchen outfitted with everything you need to create a great meal.*

Opposite—*The Glenwood, New Mexico, Dutch-oven cook-off is a family affair down to the smallest details, such as peeling potatoes.*

Shafer recalls some well-known Dutch-oven favorite recipes, like "Bear Sign," the name of a simple dish of rice cooked with raisins. "Son-of-a-Gun Stew" was made when a cow was freshly butchered. Liver, heart, sweetbreads and all edible internal parts were boiled together. In the Old West, cowboys would throw bulls' eyes right into the chile for a special bit of seasoning.

"Ranching's not a business," she says. "It's a way of life, and you raise your children in it, and they learn to love it. Dutch-oven cooking is part of that way of life. It's like any lost art—you hate to see it die out."

Somehow, ranch life would not be the same without the comfort of a good hot meal prepared outdoors over an open fire. "Everything tastes better with a little wood smoke," says Bobby Shafer, grinning over his heaping plate.

How right he is.

Parts of this chapter originally appeared in *New Mexico Magazine* in June 1996.

RECIPES

Bill Gallacher's Sheepherder Chile (Serves 4)

Brown 1½ pounds of round steak cut in squares. Add 1 large chopped onion and 3 cloves of minced garlic. Add red chile to taste: 1–2 teaspoons for starters.

Stir, cover chile with ¼ cup flour and stir again. Add water to cover. Stir in salt to taste and 1 teaspoon ground cumin. Add 1 teaspoon sugar.

Cook until meat is tender, about a half-hour, stirring often. Adjust seasonings. Serve with beans.

Jane Shafer's Arroz con Pollo (Serves 4)

Sauté 1 chopped onion with 2 large chopped garlic cloves.

Add 1 cut-up chicken; keep stirring until brown.

Add 2 cups of rice and 1 large can of V8 juice. Refill the can with water, add and keep stirring. Bring to a boil, then lower to simmer.

Add 1 cup chopped green chile, black olives if you like and green peas. Season with oregano and cumin, salt and pepper.

Add 1 teaspoon of red chile. Simmer for an hour or until rice is tender.

This dish is one of my dinner and company standbys. I serve it with beans and salad. I fix it in a Dutch oven on top of the stove.

Opposite—*Harding County's Solanofest offers a Dutch-oven cook-off that's worth the drive.*

Opposite—*The hot springs as well as the bright, vivid colors of this downtown establishment add to the allure of Truth or Consequences.*

Far left—*No one knows how long this stop sign outside of Pie Town on the Continental Divide has graced U.S. 60, but it's a roadside icon you don't want to miss.*

Left—*You can't leave Tucumcari without a visit to Tepee Curios, a Route 66 landmark. That's where you'll find keychains, T-shirts, shot glasses and all sorts of souvenirs to commemorate your journey on the Mother Road.*

Above and above, right—*With only eight picnic tables inside, El Farolito in El Rito packs in the customers who know how to appreciate the best green-chile-smothered enchiladas. A lantern in the window reflects the establishment's name. The restaurant provides the perfect stop on a Sunday drive to Abiquiú or Ojo Caliente.*

Opposite—*Stop anywhere in New Mexico, such as at this soda fountain in Cimarrón, and you can always be assured of a warm welcome to go with your old-fashioned root beer float or the more contemporary frozen cappuccino drinks.*

Above—The evocative signs of the past live on long after the doors of older establishments have closed, such as on this building in Carrizozo.

Left—Downtown Socorro preserves its history at this 19th-century landmark brick building.

Opposite—This painting on the Los Ojos Restaurant and Saloon in Jémez Springs beckons cowpokes to belly up to the bar.

Above—Cowboys park their dusty boots on the portal at the Bell Ranch in Harding County.

Left—Tío Vivo, the legendary merry-go-round, still makes an occasional appearance in Taos, thanks to the area Lions Club. Each pony was decorated a century ago by a different Taos artist.

Right—Cottonwoods spread their deep roots along the acequias of Albuquerque's North Valley. The centuries-old ditch system carries water from the Río Grande to the fields and gardens.

Above—*A vintage Buckaroo Motel neon sign lights up the night sky in Tucumcari.*

Left—*The worn Whiting Brothers sign, visible from I-40 west of Albuquerque, remains an icon of Old Route 66.*

Opposite—*The sign from the Blue Swallow Motel, a Route 66 classic, frames the Tucumcari streetscape with nostalgia.*

Below—*Open only during warm weather, the Burrito Banquet in Cimarrón is a local favorite and beloved dining spot for Boy Scouts who visit the Philmont Scout Ranch in the summer.*

Above—*The young ladies of Hatch serve cold beverages at the annual Hatch Chile Festival during the Labor Day weekend.*

Opposite—*Growers unpack and display their produce at the Taos Farmers Market. New Mexico has many wonderful outdoor markets where customers can meet the people who grow their food.*

New Mexico, in 1989, became the first state in the nation to adopt an official state cookie. With that matter put to rest, the Legislature debated the proper spelling of the revered, beloved anise-flavored shortbread cookie that appears without fail at Christmas, weddings and baptismal parties. Old-fashioned traditionalists fought for "*biscochito*," but "*bizcochito*" eventually got more votes.

The spirited legislative debate generated as much attention as the question about whether Billy the Kid is actually buried in Fort Sumner and the adoption of the official state question: "Red or green?" New Mexicans have their priorities straight. They care about their history, and they care even more about satisfying their tummies. They know they've got a good thing going because, with *bizcochitos*, they can have their history and eat it, too.

No matter how you spell it, this little cookie is as important to New Mexico's identity as adobe, chile and turquoise skies. New Mexicans proudly claim the confection as their own. Yet not everyone can bake a tasty *bizcochito*. Those who can deserve our highest regard, not only for their cookie-baking skill but also for having saved the precious *bizcochito* for another generation. And if you're lucky, or specially blessed, those who can will save you an extra plate of *bizcochitos* to take home after the party!

As you travel the state from T or C to Taos, you will find our state cookie transformed into the shapes of hearts, rounds and diamonds, depending on the time of year and the baker's whim. The texture also varies. You may be served *bizcochitos* as thick as your granddad's flapjacks or as delicate and crumbly as your grandma's piecrust. Their fragrance may whisper the slight-

est whiff of anise, while their cousins may be crunchy with anise seed. The cookies might be lightly kissed with cinnamon or glistening with a generous sugar topping. Each variation is greeted with a smile of recognition, and each is a delight to sample.

In pursuit of the best *bizcochito* recipe, I sought the wisdom and *manos* (hands) of an authentic New Mexico cookie queen. The author of cowboy cookie cookbooks and a "professional cookie decorator," Tuda Libby Crews is a seventh-generation Harding County resident. She doesn't live in the middle of nowhere. She resides on its far eastern edge.

Be assured, dear reader, that I will drive over the rainbow and back to bring you recipes for the most scrumptious New Mexican delicacies. Crews' *bizcochitos* are by far the most delectable, melt-in-your mouth native New Mexico cookies I have ever encountered. Their deep, yet not overly sweet, flavor, lightness and delicate crumbliness could inspire poems and wedding proposals. Each taste tantalizes you to reach for another cookie.

Had Marcel Proust, the author with the remarkable memory, tasted one of Crews' *bizcochitos* instead of his madeleine, French literature would have taken a different course. It likely would have turned west at the Champs-Elysées and headed for the high desert.

As my native New Mexican husband said when he sampled three of Crews' *bizcochitos* that I had saved for him, "Those are the best *bizcochitos* I ever put in my mouth, and they could be the best cookies I have ever tasted."

The talented *bizcochito* baker practices her art from the well-equipped, red-trimmed kitchen of the cozy adobe ranch house she and her husband,

Jack Crews, remodeled. She's also learned to keep a well-stocked kitchen. "I'm 47 miles from a gallon of milk," says Crews, who lives on the family's Ute Creek Cattle Company Ranch in Bueyeros.

The holidays are a special time at the ranch. "There's no Christmas without *bizcochitos*," she says. The cookies are as essential to her family's holiday meal as the *posole* (hominy and chile stew), beans, chile and their ranch-raised beef, which is prepared simply on the grill until medium rare. She serves the cookies with *natillas*, a sweet, creamy custard.

The origin of the *bizcochito* is almost as elusive as its spelling. Some claim that the cookies' heritage reaches back to 16th-century Spain, where they were known as *mantecosas*, meaning buttery. Crews suggests that the cookies may have traveled up from the South after the Civil War with the war veterans, cowhands and homesteaders as shortbread, perhaps of Scottish or British origins, and picked up their anise accent once they crossed the Río Grande. To add to the international intrigue, I have found a similar recipe for Egyptian butter cookies, minus the lard, called *ghorayebah*, in *The Book of Jewish Food: An Odyssey from Samarkand to New York*, by Claudia Roden. These favorite cookies, flavored with cardamom or cinnamon, could conceivably have Sephardic Jewish roots stretching back to the Middle East. After all, New Mexico is home to Crypto-Jewish families for whom a favorite sweet delicacy would have been a precious reminder of the past.

Today, however, you are not likely to find *bizcochitos* with their recognizable taste of butter, anise and cinnamon sugar outside of New Mexico. Not unless you happen to be lucky enough to receive a tin for the holidays from your *abuelita* (grandmother). Although the cookies do freeze and pack

well, the art of preparing them does not seem to have crossed state lines.

Crews learned the art of *bizcochito* baking from her grandmother, Isabell C. de Baca, a "fabulous cook" who, as a girl, attended the boarding school at Loretto Heights Academy in Denver.

"My earliest childhood memories are of midnight Mass, *posole* and *bizcochitos*," she says, recalling her "rich, prayerful and vivid" childhood Christmases under the tutelage of her "strict Catholic grandmother."

Like most confident, experienced cooks, Crews measures her ingredients with her hands. But on one point, she is rigorous. "You have to use the lard to get the authentic flavor and texture." Her message is clear: no Crisco allowed.

She does adapt the customary brown cinnamon topping, however, for special occasions. She decorates her *bizcochitos* at Christmas with red and green sugar, and for parties she favors hot-orange and lime-green sugar toppings.

And the shapes of her *bizcochitos*, which she sculpts with her sharp little knife, one by one, are also special. Instead of baking them in the traditional round or heart shapes, she creates fleur-de-lis and rosette patterns.

Just like Grandma taught her.

RECIPES

Tuda's Bizcochitos Yields approximately 24 cookies per sheet or 96 *bizcochitos*.

- 1 cup lard
- 1 heaping cup sugar
- 2 large eggs
- 1 teaspoon salt
- 6 teaspoons anise seed
- 6 cups flour
- 3 teaspoons baking powder
- ⅛ cup red wine
- ⅛ cup orange juice concentrate, partially thawed

Topping

- 4 teaspoons cinnamon
- ½ cup sugar

Prepare topping before rolling out dough. Lightly grease cookie sheets. Preheat oven to 350 degrees F.

At close to full speed, whip the lard until it is silky—about 5 minutes. While the mixer is operating, add sugar and beat until incorporated. Stop mixing and scrape the sides of the bowl.

Continue beating, adding eggs one by one. Combine wine and orange juice concentrate and add. Sift flour, salt and baking powder

and add. Add anise seed and mix on medium speed until dough comes away from the sides of the bowl.

Rolling out the dough between two sheets of extra-wide plastic wrap prevents it from sticking to the rolling pin (a clever trick to use with cut-out cookies and piecrust). With a wet sponge, moisten the countertop. With fingers moistened, place a sheet of plastic wrap over the damp-ened countertop (using moisture makes it easier to work with the plastic wrap).

Gently flour the surface of the plastic wrap. Re-move dough from the mixing bowl and place it on the plastic wrap. Touching the dough with the flat of your hand, shape it into a rectangle and pat it down. Place another sheet of plastic wrap over the top of the dough. Use damp-ened fingers to stretch it over the dough, allow-ing it to cling to the edges of the bottom sheet of plastic wrap.

Roll out the dough to ½-inch thickness. (Tuda prefers using a heavy marble rolling pin.)

Remove the top layer of plastic wrap. Cut the entire rectangle of dough into 1½-inch squares.

As you remove each square, dip the surface of the dough into the sugar/cinnamon topping and place each on the cookie sheet lined up about ½ inch apart.

With a small, sharp knife, make a short diagonal cut from each corner toward the center of each square.

You now have a cookie sheet of little squares with diagonal cuts on the four corners of each square. To form the traditional rosette shape, use thumbs and forefingers (both hands at the same time) on the cut corners of each square and gently pinch together while pushing inward. The shape you create resembles a small rosette with four "petals." With practice, shaping the *bizcochitos* becomes a breeze. (You may also use a cookie press or cookie cutters.)

Bake about 13 minutes or until golden brown around the edges. Tuda prefers her *bizcochitos* crisp. If they are not brown enough, return to the oven for another 2–3 minutes. The exact length of cooking time may vary from oven to oven.

Opposite—*Tuda Libby Crews' patient fingers shape each bizcochito as delicately as a piece of clay being readied for the kiln. These cookies take time, but they are so worth it.*

L iving traditions endure so long as time proves them to be the best way of accomplishing a task necessary for survival. That task may be the bonding of a tribe, or it may be a ritual surrounding the production, preparation, sharing and consumption of sustenance. When a tradition ceases to be useful, it is no longer practiced. It may remain respected, but it is no longer alive. It will either be transformed, become symbolic or be preserved in a story, legend, museum or cultural shrine. Perhaps, eventually, it will be forgotten. Baking bread in an *horno*, the "beehive" outdoor oven seen throughout New Mexico in villages and pueblos, remains very much a living tradition particularly for the Pueblo people. It provides an everyday, hands-on connection to ancestral generations that continues to be eminently practical. Tracing the *horno*, a Spanish word for oven, back to its roots, the Towa language refers to it as *belaha-tha*, which means literally "bread-baking protector," according to Pueblo historian Joe Sando.

Built of adobe and plastered with mud like a house, the traditional round-mound oven cooks by heat absorbed and radiated from its earthen walls. A wood fire is first built in the oven. Piñon wood is the traditional fuel, easily gathered locally. After the fire burns to glowing coals and the oven walls have absorbed the heat of the wood, the coals are swept from the oven and the leavened round loaves are loaded in to bake. The experienced baker judges the temperature not by a thermometer but by tossing in a piece of crumpled newspaper. If the oven is hot enough to scorch the paper immediately, it is ready for the baking process.

When the bread has baked for about 25 to 40 minutes, the crusty, golden loaves are removed with a wooden paddle, wrapped in cloth and hustled

Opposite—*Oven bread is baked in the horno exactly the same way as it has been for centuries. The Walatowa Visitor Center at Jemez Pueblo is a good place to observe the process.*

into the kitchen. The baking crew breaks a loaf of hot bread and passes it around the table. Each tears off a chunk, spreads it with butter and wild plum preserves, and makes a breakfast of bread and hot coffee poured from the old-fashioned percolator on the stove.

The scent of piñon smoke mixed with that of baking bread, particularly on a chilly winter morning, evokes all that is good and warm and familiar about home, a home anchored on the earth in the same place for countless generations. The *horno* symbolizes the beauty of being rooted to home. Not being portable, it proclaims that home—the land of the ancestors—is the chosen place to live. Indeed, photos of Taos Pueblo in the 1920s show the same *hornos*, not far from the pueblo church, that still stand today.

Baking bread in an *horno* is efficient and sustainable since it uses what is available: mud to build the oven, wood to fire the baking, and wheat grown by the farmers and watered by the Río Grande. The female members of the tribe mill, winnow and grind the wheat. Bread, the staff of life, is baked by women, the providers of life.

Unexpectedly, while on a recent trip to Egypt, I found rural women not far from the Valley of the Kings cooking in round adobe ovens shaped exactly like New Mexico *hornos*. They produced a crusty bread almost identical to Pueblo oven bread. This similarity makes perfect sense, as the *horno* was introduced to the Iberian Peninsula by the Moors and was subsequently brought to New Spain, now New Mexico, by the Spanish four centuries ago.

This adobe oven has neither been modified nor improved upon in a millennium. Impervious to new technology, neither the Industrial Age nor the Computer Age has made the slightest impression on its form or function.

Contemporary Pueblo bakers in New Mexico still prepare oven bread; fruit pies cut in square servings and stuffed with prune, peach or apricot; *chicos* (dried corn); and even entire meals, including roast turkeys, in the *horno*.

Since the *horno* accommodates large quantities, it is ideal for feasts and ceremonies. Its use at such events, and the tasks associated with preparing for its use—gathering and chopping wood as well as planting, tending, harvesting, winnowing and milling wheat and corn—support the continuity of the community. The substance of which the oven is made—simple earth—and its sensuous form, along with the quantities of food generated from this brilliantly simple outdoor appliance, suggest the productive fecundity of Mother Nature, the great and generous provider.

I have baked oven bread at dawn with Pueblo women at Taos and Isleta pueblos. Characteristically, the dough is mixed, kneaded and set to rise the evening before baking is to take place. It is a sourdough bread, risen from starter. The next morning, loaves are formed and arranged on enormous baking sheets. The fire is built at dawn, and as the sun radiates its warmth, the loaves are loaded into the oven. Often the women of an extended

Fall weekends are an excellent time to drive to Jemez Pueblo and sample the fry bread. Piled high with beans and red chile, an Indian taco provides a hearty meal.

family gather together for these tasks, joking and sharing the labor that provides this most basic form of sustenance. The coordinated movements of the bakers have the power of a ritual. Bread is always baked the same way, incorporating lessons passed on and learned.

In his ethnographic account, *Zuni Breadstuff*, Frank Hamilton Cushing, who lived at Zuni during the 1880s and earned sufficient respect to become second chief of the tribe, describes the ritual of baking bread in the *horno* as vividly as anyone ever has:

> *"The dough loaves are laid on flat stones or boards and taken to the oven which has been cleared meanwhile of its fire, swept out and scented with cedar leaves, and passed in by means of a long-handled shovel of pine, usually quite handsomely carved. As soon as the oven is full, the vent-hole at the top is plugged, the doorway closed with a heavy stone and plastered and the bread left baking for the space of from twenty minutes to half an hour, or under certain circumstances, a longer time. Then the stone is taken down and loaves shoveled out. They are crisp, brown, and very light, having almost doubled in size during the baking. The bread is hearty and nutritious, although inclined to be slightly sour if overleavened."*

You can actually build an *horno* in your own backyard. Should you wish, you can observe and learn *horno* bread baking at Petroglyph National Monument in Albuquerque, Fort Selden State Monument and the Wala-towa Visitor Center at Jemez Pueblo.

Opposite—*These Zuni Pueblo youths gather for a festive summer celebration.*

This Pueblo youngster is eager to sample some of the delicious oven bread that his mother has just baked.

Drive along any two-lane road in northern New Mexico, keep your eyes open, and you are likely to find fresh-baked oven bread, usually arrayed on the back of a pickup truck. It may also be for sale under the Palace of the Governors' Portal in Santa Fe, along with Indian-made jewelry, or in convenience stores, produce stores and from vendors along the road to Gallup or Chaco Canyon. You might also find it in front of Albuquerque supermarkets and at farmers markets, gas stations, roadside stands, festivals, powwows and Pueblo dances.

The bread's shape and loft make it excellent for toast, French toast or scooping up gravy from a bowl of stew. It is especially delicious with butter, local honey or homemade preserves. Expect to pay from $3 to $6 for a loaf. Wherever you taste it, you will find the flavor remarkably consistent from loaf to loaf. Chew each bite slowly, savoring the wood and wheat scents, the agility and deftness of human hands, the sanctity and sustainability of authentic tradition.

RECIPE

Oven Bread at Home (2 loaves)

1 package dry yeast
½ cup shortening
¼ cup honey or sugar
½ teaspoon salt
1 cup warm water
4 cups all-purpose flour

Dissolve yeast in ¼ cup of warm water. Mix and set aside.

Mix shortening, honey or sugar, and salt in a large bowl. Add 1 cup very warm water and stir well. When the mixture cools to room temperature, mix well with the yeast.

Add 4 cups of flour, stirring well after each cup.

Knead dough on a floured surface until it is softened (about 15 minutes). Place dough in a large bowl, cover with cloth and put in a warm place until dough doubles in size. Knead again.

Divide dough into 2 equal parts. Shape each into a loaf. Place the loaves on a well-greased cookie sheet, cover with cloth and allow them to rise in a warm place.

Place loaves in an oven preheated to 400 degrees F and bake until lightly browned (about 1 hour). Use the oven's middle rack and place a shallow pan of water on the bottom of the oven.

This recipe yields 2 loaves of sweet-smelling oven bread. Enjoy it with a bowl of green-chile stew or with butter.

The above recipe is used at the Petroglyph National Monument in Albuquerque during baking demonstrations given in the cooler months.

very Labor Day weekend, the village of Hatch, New Mexico, population approximately 2,000, steps up to defend its proud title as Chile Capital of the World. During that weekend, the town's tiny population grows to 20,000; visitors swarm the place to take part in the heated mayhem that is the Hatch Chile Festival. Part harvest ritual, part country fair, part chowhound heaven, the festival is the state's hottest ticket.

The celebration of all things chile goes on all weekend with chile-eating contests, a classic parade, the coronation of the Chile Queen, and roasting, roasting and more roasting. From dawn to dusk, the *ka-woosh* of propane-fired roasters is heard as they charge up, charring the skins of freshly harvested chiles and emanating the aroma that is the chile lover's aphrodisiac. On this weekend, chile lovers go from one grower's booth to the next, tasting until they find the one chile that enflames their senses, the one they must have. Forty-pound burlap sacks of chiles are selected, dumped into the roaster and then licked to perfection by the blue gas flame and poured back into the sacks to be transported to Albuquerque, Amarillo, Tularosa and Tempe.

Driving south on I-25, lush green fields shine beside the roadway as it leads south into Doña Ana County. Beside a crook in the Río Grande, the road veers right near exit 41, the Hatch exit. The first settlement on this well watered site, Santa Barbara, dates to 1851. In 1875, the growing village took the name of Hatch, for General Edward Hatch, commander of nearby Fort Thorn. It was renamed Hatch's Station when the Atchison, Topeka & Santa Fe Railway came through in the 1880s.

It would have remained another small agricultural village, producing cotton, corn, onions and subsistence crops, but for the development of com-

Opposite—The Mesilla Valley, in southern New Mexico, produces much of the state's legendary green chile, which, when left in the fields to ripen, transforms into red chile.

Chiles Rellenos Soufflé (Serves 4)

An easy way to enjoy the taste of *chiles rellenos* without the frying. A delicious slight tweak of tradition. Makes a wonderful brunch dish.

> 6 eggs, separated
> 1 cup milk
> 2 tablespoons butter
> ¼ cup flour
> ½ teaspoon salt
> 2 cups grated sharp cheddar cheese
> 12 good-sized Hatch green chiles, seeded and peeled
> 1 pound Colby cheese, sliced

Preheat oven to 475 degrees F. Get all ingredients to room temperature. Butter a soufflé pan or any ovenproof dish with high sides.

Slice each chile lengthwise and stuff each with a slice of Colby cheese. Layer them in the soufflé pan.

Melt butter in a saucepan. Add flour. Stir for 3 minutes on low. Add milk, stirring constantly, until the mixture thickens.

Add grated cheddar to the sauce slowly, allowing it to melt, and keep stirring with a whisk until all the cheese is melted. Turn off heat.

Beat egg yolks 2 minutes on high until fluffy. Beat whites until they form fluffy meringue-like peaks, about 4 minutes on high.

Return saucepan to heat. Gently fold in egg yolks. Then gently fold in beaten egg whites. Pour sauce over stuffed chiles in the soufflé pan.

Place in the middle of the oven for 10 minutes. Lower heat to 400 degrees F. Bake for 20 minutes more. The soufflé should be firm, airy and golden brown. Serve immediately with hot garlic bread and salad.

mercial chile growing fostered by nearby New Mexico State University (NMSU) in Las Cruces. So it was that Hatch became the primary producer of the state's largest agricultural crop, the very crop that became New Mexico's trademark.

At one time, 30,000 acres were in production here, and chile was unquestionably New Mexico's biggest cash crop. Since the advent of NAFTA, however, that number has fallen to 11,000 cultivated acres, as local farmers struggle to compete with lower-priced foreign-grown chile. Adding to the struggle in recent years are the big floods, damaging homes and crops in a low-lying area prone to flooding.

An abundance of crimson chile ristras signals the fall harvest season in Hatch.

Hatch chile has its mystique, although there really is no strain known as "Hatch chile." Chile is sold in Hatch as mild, medium, hot and extra hot. What is termed Hatch chile is reputed to be the meatiest and most flavorful. These chiles, however, developed at NMSU's Chile Pepper Institute, are actually varieties of the Anaheim pepper that include New Mexico 6-4, introduced in 1957, and Big Jim, introduced in 1975. Sandía chiles may also be in the mix. Renewed strains of these chiles, more flavorful and aromatic, are now coming on line.

Above—*Packing a sack of hot, fragrant green chiles fresh from the propane-powered roaster is a team sport.*

Opposite—*Selecting your own chiles at the Hatch Chile Festival gives you an opportunity to taste-test the product as well as meet the growers.*

Regardless, there is nothing like making a pilgrimage to Hatch to stock up during chile season. If you love chile, you need to get it while it's hot—fresh and bursting with flavor—because the season is short and the good chile goes fast. No real New Mexican wants to be without a freezer full of Hatch green chile to get through the winter. What is winter without green-chile stew, *chiles rellenos*, enchiladas, *queso* and salsa? Once you have acquired a taste for green chile, a plain cheeseburger, grilled-cheese sandwich or cheese omelette without chile is unpalatable. When you have become truly addicted, you will think about putting chile on everything, from lasagna to lox and bagels. Only the morning bowl of oatmeal will remain a chile-free zone.

Come to think of it, just to make life interesting, you really need to take home at least two sacks of roasted Hatch green chile.

The recipe on page 94 will give you an idea of how we get through the northern New Mexico winter at our house. Chile dishes are particularly delicious with hot tortillas. When we can sit in front of a toasty fire and eat chile, we don't mind getting snowed in one bit.

There is, in southern New Mexico, one café that everyone knows; the place is as legendary as the food. People don't make the pilgrimage here for the faux wood-paneled decor; rather, they return for the feeling of eating in Grandma's kitchen. In a world where uncertainty rules, Chope's Bar & Café never changes. Count on it.

Everyone who has lived here has eaten here, and so have their parents, their grandparents and their cousins from California. There may be arguments around the table about whether the red or the green chile is better, or if the salsa used to be hotter. The tender *chiles rellenos*, it is agreed, are the best to be found anywhere, and the blazing *chile con queso*, served with fresh, hot tortillas, is notorious, in a good way. Bring the red enchiladas into the picture, and tough choices have to be made.

Hot weather and the chile harvest, with the aroma of peppers roasting in the air, inspire anyone with half an ounce of New Mexican blood to crave the piquant flavor that brings tears to the eyes and sweat to the brow. Chope's satisfies the most discerning aficionados of pepper power.

Even (or especially) on a 100-degree-plus August morning, folks from Las Cruces to El Paso line up, anticipating the opening of this modest little roadside café. Chope's is open Tuesday through Saturday and closed on Sunday and Monday.

Las Cruces may be the New Orleans of New Mexican cuisine, with many legendary establishments to inspire love and loyalty, but no other local café has the tacos and enchiladas to command a lunchtime line. Chope's is 14 miles south of Old Mesilla on gently curving N.M. 28, in La Mesa, one of the picturesque little farming villages strung along this historic two-lane road

Opposite—*Chope's Bar & Café, approaching its seventh decade in operation, remains a must-visit destination for generations of New Mexico food aficionados.*

Opposite—*The restaurant remains in the family, with Chope's daughters cooking in the café's tiny kitchen, using recipes handed down for generations.*

that shine in the sun like precious jewels that have been in the family forever. Each home is well-kept, cared for and preserved for the next generation.

This is the road Juan de Oñate led his conquistadors along at the turn of the 16th century. The drive is one of New Mexico's most scenic, with a shady roadway that crisscrosses the Río Grande, passing by Stahmann's 4,000-treed acres, the largest family-owned pecan grove in the world, planted in the 1930s. Then it rolls past green chile and onion fields, bordered by the jagged Organ Mountains. Tidy, well-tended little houses offer goats, fresh eggs, *remedios*, fortunes and, of course, chile. This area, south of booming Las Cruces from Mesilla onward, wears a timeless feel—like a soft, hand-knit shawl.

Generations live here beside the Río Grande, tending their farms and their animals—growing and preserving within the family and the church community, giving each season its due, and celebrating each fiesta and holiday together.

For more than a half-century, Chope's, with its everlasting charm, has served as a central gathering place for these families of farmers, as well as students from New Mexico State University, Las Cruces business people, visitors and politicians. Going back still further, food made from local ingredients has been served on this spot since 1915. Chope's mother, Longina Benavides, first made and sold tamales to the local farmers out of her La Mesa house. Her tradition was to hang a kerosene lantern outside the front door when the tamales were ready.

Chope Benavides, well known in these parts as a proud Democrat, built a bar next door to the home he inherited in 1940 and, in 1948, Chope's

restaurant, as we know it today, opened its doors. This well-known chile parlor is still in the family, now owned by Chope's three daughters—Cecilia Llanez, Amelia Rivas and Margie Martinez. And it is still a home. Doña Lupe, Chope's widow, going on 90-plus years, still lives in the back of the restaurant.

Chope's exists in two sections. The restaurant is a small house where a busy kitchen staff is visible chopping onions, grating cheese and rolling enchiladas on a formica kitchen table, like so many *abuelitas*. Every order is prepared by hand, as it always has been. Cooking methods, which have been passed down through generations, are done by feel, not by recipe. For example, the lady who prepares the famous *chiles rellenos* has worked here 23 years and, before that, her mother made the same dish. Despite the volume of business done here, this still looks and feels like granny's kitchen. There's nothing commercial about it.

To the north, usually with a cadre of motorcycles parked out front, is the original Chope's, in a separate building housing the dark, narrow bar. Here, in the olden days, many a deal was completed. On Friday nights, when the margaritas and the beer are flowing, mariachis wail the melancholy of Mexican soul. It is not a sound—or a scene—to be missed.

Chope's is at 16145 S. N.M. 28 in La Mesa.

RECIPE

Chope's Chiles Rellenos

12 firm, long green chiles
1 pound yellow Longhorn cheese
¾ cup flour
2 cups pure lard
4 eggs, separated

Roast green chiles on a hot stove grill. Peel the chiles.

Cut 12 strips of cheese, making each strip 3 to 4 inches long and ½-inch square in thickness.

Make a ½-inch cut on one side near the top of each chile and insert the cheese strip. Dredge the stuffed chiles in flour until well coated. Set aside.

In a deep skillet, melt the lard and heat to medium hot. (Eggs will burn if the lard is too hot.) Keep the burner set on medium.

Beat 4 egg whites until they form peaks. Add egg yolks and beat for ½ minute.

Dip floured chile in egg batter until well coated and fry until golden brown. Drain well and serve warm.

(This recipe first appeared in *New Mexico Magazine* in August 1981.)

Opposite—*The inviting Frito pie (above) or a plate of smothered green enchiladas with frijoles on the side are among the most popular items on the menu at Chope's.*

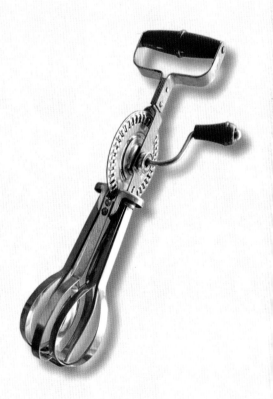

As people with New Mexico roots can tell you, chokecherry season arrives in mid- to late-August. That's when families head out to the hills and stream banks to fill their buckets with the tiny, garnet berries that make a sweet-tangy jelly (a rare delicacy) or a deep rose-colored wine or liqueur that takes the chill off winter evenings. The trick is to find the berries—smaller than a Bing cherry by about half, with about twice as much pit—while they are hanging in clusters ripe on the tree before the bears and the birds have taken them all.

Throughout New Mexico, from Cimarrón Canyon to the Manzano Mountains, families forage for the wild cherry, one of the most widespread edible and medicinal native plants in North America. It is found throughout New England, along the Appalachian Trail and the Eastern Seaboard and into Missouri, Kansas, Iowa, New Mexico and Colorado. As a pioneer species, the chokecherry thrives in open sites with rich, moist soils. Because birds distribute the seeds, the tree takes root on the borders of woods, in clearings, and along creek and ditch banks.

Many New Mexico families return to their chokecherry trees season after season for wildcrafting. The slender, shrublike tree, a member of the rose family with the botanical name of *Prunus virginiana*, rarely grows taller than 30 feet. Small white flowers appear on its branches in the spring, maturing months later into prized berries. Sour enough when raw to produce a hard pucker, which is how the berry got its name, the chokecherry's astringent taste mellows out when it is dried or cooked.

Stan Schug, associate curator of horticulture at the Río Grande Botanical Garden in Albuquerque, says the wild chokecherry can be cultivated in

Above—*Raton backyards yield their chokecherry harvest to those willing to reach the highest.*

Opposite—*The trick to successfully foraging for chokecherries in Cimarrón Canyon is to find them when they are ripe enough for picking, before the bears beat you to it.*

RECIPES

Chokecherry Juice

Wash chokecherries thoroughly and clean well, removing stems and leaves.

Cover with water and boil until soft.

Remove pits and skins from boiled chokecherries by running them through a sieve. Tightly wrap the pulp in cheesecloth. Hang over a pot overnight to obtain the remaining juice.

Chokecherry Jelly (Makes 6 jars)

This Certo gelatin recipe was used by Eloise Henry of Raton for at least 50 years.

    3 cups prepared chokecherry juice
    6½ cups sugar
    2 pouches (6 ounces) Certo gelatin

Add the juice to the sugar. Mix well. Stir constantly on high heat. Bring to a full rolling boil that continues while you stir.

Add the Certo all at once while you keep stirring. Bring to a full rolling boil again. Allow to boil for 1 minute. Remove from heat. Skim off the foam.

Pour the hot liquid through a funnel into sterilized jars placed on a tray. Seal and store.

Chokecherry Liqueur (Makes 2 quarts)

Excerpted from *The Rocky Mountain Wild Foods Cookbook* by Darcy Williamson (Caxton Press, 1995), this liqueur dressed in a fun bottle makes a perfect gift.

    1 teaspoon freshly grated nutmeg
    1 teaspoon freshly grated allspice
    7 pounds chokecherries made into juice
    4 cups sugar (or to taste)
    3 cups water
    2 cups rum
    2 cups brandy

Strain prepared chokecherry juice through several layers of cheesecloth.

Add sugar and spices to juice and bring to a boil; simmer 3 to 4 minutes. Allow to stand overnight. Strain again.

Add rum and brandy and stir well. Store in a cool, dark place in a covered crock for a month or 2 or decant directly into bottles and seal with corks.

home gardens. "I like to use them as a bird attractant," he says. The chokecherry prefers indirect light and rich soil that is at least 50 percent compost. Purchase the trees at native plant nurseries and keep them out of full, direct sun.

CHERRY VARIETIES

The hardy native chokecherry is found virtually throughout North America. Different varieties dominate the various geographic regions.

One variety, the Western chokecherry (*Prunus virginiana var. demissa*)—a Pacific Coast native—thrives from the Sierra Nevada throughout the Great Basin region and the northern Rockies. It is found throughout the Southwest—in New Mexico, Arizona and Texas—the Midwest and in the Western states of California, Nevada, Oregon and Washington. Not surprisingly, the Western chokecherry has evolved as a heat- and drought-tolerant small tree, growing rapidly to attain a height from 20 to 30 feet. Two similar species are the black cherry (*Prunus serotina*) and the American plum (*Prunus americana*).

A tree for all seasons, the chokecherry is lovely in spring, with slender, delicate clusters of fragrant white flowers that develop into deep-red berries by mid-August. One of the most important woody plant fruits for wildlife, the chokecherry will attract birds, butterflies and bees to the garden. The berries of *Prunus virginiana var. melanocarpa* are black, while the *Xanthocarpa* are yellow. The chokecherry's elliptical leaves make for pretty fall foliage, yielding color from bright red to pale yellow.

Although the chokecherry has a short lifespan—only about 25 years—a variety that does well in Southwestern gardens is Canada Red (*Prunus virginiana var. 'Canada Red'*). As its leaves mature during the growing season,

Wash chokecherries thoroughly and clean well, removing stems and leaves. Cover with water and boil until soft.

Remove pits and skins from boiled chokecherries by running them through a sieve. Use the rosy juice to make chokecherry jelly or liqueur (recipes on page 106).

Sometimes it takes a little help from a friend who likes to oversee the jelly-making process.

they turn from green to crimson. This variety may be sensitive to wind damage, however, and likes to have its leaves sprayed with a fish-kelp fertilizer. It needs a rich, moist soil to simulate its natural stream bank habitat.

During the winter, its slender trunk and twisting branches reveal a smooth-grained bark, a shade between gray and brown, creating a point of interest in the garden. The wood, while hard, is not valued for commercial use due to its small diameter and irregular trunk.

The healing and nutritive properties of the chokecherry are well-known to Native people. Meriwether Lewis, taken ill during the Lewis and Clark Expedition, was revived by drinking a tea prepared of wild cherry bark (Sacagawea's recipe, perhaps?). A staple Indian food, pemmican, is made by grinding dried chokecherries, pits and all, with pulverized meat and fat, then baked to form a jerky that stores and travels well. The Indian diet, rich in vitamin C-loaded berries, prevented scurvy.

An infusion of the mature black bark is thought to be a remedy for headaches, fevers, worms, diarrhea, sore throats, coughs, bronchitis and heart problems. It is also used as an eyewash. The cherry bark tea was sipped in the springtime by Indians, homesteaders and mountain people as a cleansing spring tonic.

Hispanic old-timers in the Manzanos tell of a favorite dessert made by pouring chokecherry syrup over fresh goat cheese and then lightly broiling it. This dish could have originated as an interpretation of the fruit-and-cheese combination eaten as a last course in Spain, a resourceful way to use whatever was available.

"People who knew how to manage had their chickens and cows and hogs and a beef to butcher. Some of them say they remember going hungry, that they just lived on cornmeal and mush or something like that. But I think very few people had to live that way."
—Homesteader Francis Beebe of Portales

Express Mail now delivers fresh ingredients to top chefs from anywhere in the world overnight. Meanwhile, the rest of us can usually purchase whatever exotic ingredients we desire off grocery shelves.

Thanks to overnight shipping, "out of season" no longer applies to asparagus, mangos and fresh berries, and our appetites for new and unusual flavors expand along with the increasing availability of ingredients.

Those who live in or near metropolitan centers can obtain just about any ingredient needed or desired for any recipe to wow guests at the next dinner party. But what happened decades ago, when ranching families who lived a hundred miles from town had to feed 15 with whatever they had on hand?

Those pioneers got creative. Their cooking matched their philosophy of living. They grew and raised what they could, used what they had, such as flour from 100-pound sacks, and wasted nothing, not even the drippings from fried meat. They dipped into stores of preserved foods, such as sauerkraut, to come up with tasty and nourishing meals to feed hungry families and workers.

"We couldn't get lemons or limes, so we made vinegar pie," says Genora Moore, formerly of Galisteo, who grew up on a ranch in West Texas. "Grandmother had a big garden, no electricity and she always cooked on a wood

Opposite—Abandoned homesteads in Harding County remind us how tough life was during the Pioneer era. The West is full of stories about people who learned how to survive by their wits and how to stay strong during good times and bad.

No one has yet improved upon the basic design of the windmill, and this one, on the T-4 Ranch in Montoya, still faithfully pumps water for the livestock.

stove. Mother always had a pot of beans on the stove, and we ate that good, thick bean juice over bread."

With no eggs, butter or milk due to rationing, the "whacky cake," which called for cocoa powder and oil for flavoring, was a popular treat during World War II.

"We had our beef and our staples, but it was sweets and desserts we craved," says Moore, who compiled the New Mexico CowBelles cookbook, *Enchanted Eating*, which contains many old-time recipes. (The CowBelles is an organization of women ranchers and those who support local agriculture and rural communities.)

Another believer in old-fashioned cooking is Irma Bailey, an Albuquerque Indian arts dealer, who was born in 1916 on a ranch her folks homesteaded 40 miles north of Clovis. She remembers the Dust Bowl days well.

"My father had a brand-new Buick, which I drove to my music lesson in Amarillo, a hundred miles away. On the way back, the dust came up so bad that by the time we got home, it took the paint off that Buick. Even in our solid rock house, we'd have to wear masks, and our faces would be black. It would go for days and days. I don't know how we survived.

"My father had a big smokehouse and cured his own meat, so we had lots of ham. We had our big meals at noon. The men who worked with the cattle liked redeye gravy best. Mother did lots of baking, rolls and biscuits, on a great big wood and coal stove she'd mastered, and redeye gravy went well with it.

"We had no refrigeration, so when they butchered the beef, he would hang a side of beef on the windmill tower. He covered it to keep it cold, and if Mother wanted a steak or roast, he would lower it, slice it, and back up it would go on the pulley."

Joyce Shaw, whose family homesteaded east of Mountainair in 1917, remembers her mother's pinto-bean pie. "We had our own milk and butter and eggs, and our own beans. We made this pie in winter, when we didn't have fruit from after pumpkin season into early spring. The family really liked it."

Chuck Henry's grandparents, Doc and Betsy Henry, homesteaded in Taos Junction after World War I before moving to Raton. "They looked forward to red flannel hash," a simple but pretty and tasty dish of beets, potatoes and onions, he says.

"They talked about it fondly. They could fix it in the spring as soon as the beets were ready. It went well with biscuits. My dad was quite a biscuit maker. He swore that when he made a biscuit, you had to have a rope tying it to a table, otherwise it would fly off."

RECIPES

Dorothy Cole's Sauerkraut Chocolate Cake

2 cups flour
2 eggs
1 cup buttermilk
1 cup boiling water
1 teaspoon vanilla
2 cups sugar
½ cup cocoa
1 teaspoon soda
½ teaspoon salt
1 cup drained and rinsed sauerkraut

Mix all ingredients, except water and vanilla.

Add water and vanilla; mix. The batter will be thin. Stir in sauerkraut.

Pour into 3 8-inch cake pans. Bake at 350 degrees F for 30–35 minutes. Frost with your favorite chocolate frosting.

Doc and Betsy's Red Flannel Hash (Serves 2)

3 good-sized beets
1 baking potato
1 medium onion
Salt and pepper to taste
2 tablespoons olive oil
3 cloves garlic, minced
1 teaspoon sugar

Heat oven to 425 degrees F. Spray a baking pan with nonstick spray.

Wash but do not peel beets. Roast 1¼ hours or until you can pierce with a fork. (Roasting the beets brings out the sweetness. You may also boil them until tender.) Let beets cool. Peel. Cut into ½-inch cubes.

Peel potato and cube in ½-inch cubes.

Dice onion. Heat olive oil in a heavy skillet. Sauté onions and garlic until translucent. Remove from the skillet.

Sauté potato about 10 minutes.

Return onion to pan; add beets. Cover and let steam. Salt and pepper to taste. Add sugar, mix and cover. Let steam 1–2 minutes to glaze.

Serve with fried eggs or add diced smoked turkey or ham.

Irma Bailey's Redeye Gravy (Serves 4)

Take 2 pounds of thick-sliced ham. Fry it up. Remove from skillet.

Add 1½ cups of strong black coffee to the same skillet. Stir well and serve over biscuits with fried eggs if desired.

Opposite left—*Indian trader Irma Bailey prepares redeye gravy just the way she was taught when growing up on a homestead outside Clovis during Dust Bowl days.*

Opposite right—*Red flannel hash was a favorite meal of Taos Junction homesteaders Doc and Betsy Henry.*

The Kit Carson Museum in Rayado displays an authentic storage room of goods and supplies, resembling the staples shipped across the Santa Fe Trail.

Joyce Shaw's Pinto Bean Pie

1¼ cups cooked pinto beans
1¼ cups sugar
¼ teaspoon allspice
¼ teaspoon nutmeg
½ teaspoon cinnamon
2 eggs, beaten
⅓ cup milk
¼ stick margarine, melted
1 teaspoon vanilla

Mash beans; mix in spices. Let sit overnight in refrigerator.

Add remaining ingredients; mix well.

Bake in a 9-inch unbaked pie shell 50–55 minutes at 350 degrees F.

Grandmother's Vinegar Pie

Custard:

2 egg yolks
1 cup sugar
3 heaping tablespoons flour
⅓ teaspoon salt
2 tablespoons butter
2 cups water
¼ cup vinegar

Beat egg yolks well and add water.

Combine sugar, salt and flour and add to the mixture. Add butter.

Cook over medium heat, stirring constantly, until thick and smooth.

Pour into a baked pastry shell.

Meringue:

2 egg whites
6 tablespoons sugar
1 teaspoon lemon flavoring
¼ teaspoon cream of tartar

Beat egg whites and lemon flavoring until soft peaks form. Add cream of tartar and sugar and beat to form stiff but not dry peaks.

Spread on top of the pie and brown in the oven at 325 degrees F.

From *New Mexico CowBelles' Enchanted Eating*

At age 79, Anna Clisto still lives the traditional Navajo way. In a far corner of the reservation, she tends her small flock of sheep, grows her own corn and cooks on a wood fire. Her outside kitchen is a jerry-rigged affair of corrugated tin and recycled, unrecognizable machine parts. This way of life suits her. Although she had a kidney replaced a few years back, she has no trouble climbing on top of her house to repair the roof. She is spry enough to track down a lamb that strayed into the hills above her home or to forage for the wild plants she uses to brew tea and make household utensils. And she is strong enough to chop her own wood.

So many extended family members, including children and teenagers, come and go from her kitchen that it is not always easy to tell who is visiting and who is living with her at any given time. A car horn honks. Her grandchildren rush out of the house to load into the waiting station wagon. They're on their way to attend Saturday basketball games, radio blaring as they jolt off across the wash.

Clisto dresses the same way her mother did, in broomstick skirts and kerchief, wearing her family wealth—her turquoise squash blossom necklace—every day. She still speaks only her native tongue. There is always someone around to translate for visitors.

It is clear that she is one of the last of her kind. Her life extends to the wide horizon of red mesas and radiant blue sky. Within this realm, she is a master of survival. She would smile at the outside world's talk of sustainability, renewable energy, green living, recycling and respect for the earth. What these concepts hint at is the yearning for completeness and connections to the land and family. It is something Clisto experiences every day. She

Above—*Each tortilla is lovingly kneaded and shaped by hand before it is baked.*

Opposite—*At 79, Anna Clisto still lives the traditional Navajo way, tending her sheep and her land, growing her own food and feeding her family with meals cooked over the open fire.*

Anna Clisto stirs boiling water with strong "stirring sticks" she made from cactus stems she gathered from the hill above her home.

uses only what she has, and she knows she has whatever she needs to nourish herself, her flocks and her family. Her kind face reflects the peace of this wisdom.

The tragic story of Clisto's people is her own. She is only two generations removed from a devastating chapter in the Navajo people's history. In 1863, Army Col. Christopher (Kit) Carson and his men entered Canyon de Chelly, her people's homeland. They burned the homes, stole the livestock, destroyed the crops and peach orchards of the Diné (Navajos), and took the people into captivity. In March 1864, soldiers forced the 6,600 Navajos to go on the arduous 400-mile "Long March" to Bosque Redondo at Fort Sumner where they were detained. Hundreds died along the way. The children were taken and sent away to Indian schools where they were punished for speaking their own language. Removed from their accustomed food sources and way of life, many detainees starved or grew ill and died.

With the signing of a peace treaty in June 1868, those who survived were sent back to the Navajo Reservation, 3.5 million acres of their former homeland that stretches in checkerboard fashion through northwestern New Mexico and northeastern Arizona. Miraculously, their spiritual paths, their stories, their agriculture and their relationships to the land and animals survived.

Clisto still cooks traditional foods in the old way. She adds fine-ground roasted blue corn to boiling water over a wood fire to prepare a nutritious cornmeal mush. She planted, grew and harvested the corn herself. Traditional rituals and blessings regulate the cultivation of this crop. Corn is holy to the Diné; it figures prominently in their creation story.

She mixes flour and water to make tortillas and shapes them with her still-agile hands. Their aroma, steaming on the hot griddle over the crackling fire, is delicious. Her diet of beans, blue corn and tortillas, supplemented with a little meat and eggs from her chickens, is simple and hearty. Her needs are few. She has running water, an electric stove, a television and a radio, tuned to the Navajo station. Her home is filled with family photos, her children's and grandchildren's trophies and award certificates, and handmade gifts from family members. Her pantry is stocked with staples of coffee, hominy and crackers.

Clisto lives amidst the blazing beauty of the desert; she is as rooted to this place as the 200-year-old cedars that grow beside her home.

RECIPES

Anna's Blue Corn Mush

Boil a pot of water.

Fill a bowl with cold water and a tablespoon of cedar ash. Mix well.

Stir roasted blue corn meal into the bowl slowly, adding a handful at a time.

Slowly add the mixture of corn meal and cedar ash to the boiling water. Add more corn meal for a thicker consistency.

Stir constantly for 10-15 minutes.

Serve plain or with sugar.

Like beans sprouting after a good May morning rain, farmers markets have taken root in New Mexico from Aztec to Tularosa. These outdoor markets provide fresh fruit and vegetables for the kitchen and a joyous community spirit for the heart. From the appearance of the first new greens of spring until the frosty mornings of the October pumpkin harvest, more than 50 farmers markets in towns large and small bring growers together with buyers eager for fresh produce direct from the fields.

Farmers markets feel like parties—social gatherings complete with live music where you can meet friends, catch up on the news and find out what's happening in the neighborhood.

New Mexico truly is a big small town, which is evident in the camaraderie found in parks and parking lots where growers set up their stands of fresh sweet corn, apples, squash and melons early on Saturday mornings. Neighbors gather at card tables to sip coffee and munch breakfast burritos, while children play and grown-ups scurry to get the first tomatoes and peaches. Jams, jellies and chutneys made from native and foraged chokecherries, wild plums, currants and raspberries—often blended with chile— are abundant. Wildflower honeys and beauty products crafted from locally grown lavender and sage add to the markets' intoxicating fragrances. Outrageously gorgeous bouquets of hot pink and orange zinnias and sunflowers, plants for the house and garden, fresh-baked breads and pastries, and chile wreaths make each market a sensual feast.

Some markets remain open all year long, including those in Santa Fe, Los Alamos, Las Cruces and Los Ranchos de Albuquerque. During the winter months, displays of handmade items provide an ongoing bazaar of irre-

Opposite—*Los Ranchos de Albuquerque's Growers Market is one of several farmers markets in the state that is open all year.*

RECIPES

Toasted Garlic Spaghetti Sauce

Heat 2 tablespoons olive oil in a heavy skillet over medium-low flame.

Peel and slice individual cloves from 3–4 medium heads of fresh garlic. Sauté garlic in oil gently, turning often, until soft and golden. Be careful not to brown, or garlic will become bitter.

Add 2 cups diced fresh tomatoes, ½ cup chopped fresh parsley, ½ cup chopped fresh basil leaves, ½ cup white wine, ½ teaspoon sugar and ½ teaspoon freshly ground black pepper. Mix well.

Cover and let simmer on low flame 10–15 minutes. Turn off heat and add ¾ cup freshly grated parmesan cheese.

Serve over hot angel hair or other pasta of your choice. Use more grated cheese for topping.

sistible goods. Dried-flower arrangements, hand-dyed silk scarves, pottery, mosaics, carved birdhouses, beaded jewelry, glasswork, hand-knitted hats, paintings and photographs are some of the wonderful one-of-a-kind gifts you'll find at the markets.

Both the numbers of producers and buyers continue to climb. Here concerns for freshness, safety, nutrition and the environment meet with the trend for urban gardens, and everybody wins. The ethos of the day is, "Think globally, act locally," and nowhere is this precept more avidly celebrated than at New Mexico's growers markets.

In Raton where I live, we are proud of the fledgling Historic First Street Growers Market. It began with a single grower, a local rancher who put up a table one July Saturday afternoon under a shady tree fronting an antique shop. She quickly sold out her supply of green beans and zucchini. The following summer, growers from Angel Fire, Maxwell and Cimarrón brought in their wares. More residents brought crops from greenhouses and gardens. Tables now line the block, and the Saturday afternoon growers market is an event people don't want to miss. Plans are in the works for a community garden, too, a place where people will grow and tend their squash and corn together in a 21st-century adaptation of the commons.

Well-established farmers markets continue to expand. In Las Cruces, the Saturday morning market, which extends along many blocks on both sides of the downtown mall, features the produce of the Mesilla Valley in addition to an extraordinary show of crafts and condiments. The Santa Fe Farmers Market provides the shopper with all the basics for a fantastic home-cooked meal, in addition to the chance to experiment with heirloom tomatoes and impress Saturday night dinner guests with "baby" squash and eggplant. Who knew potatoes came in purple, blue and so many colors of red and gold?

When fruit and vegetables are so fresh and full of flavor, they don't need much preparation to bring out the best in them. I wait all year for my special appetizer—fresh basil and a slice of red ripe tomato atop a slice of fresh mozarella cheese, drizzled with olive oil. For entertaining, or just enjoying a summer afternoon on the deck, this chapter offers a few of my recipes for simple dishes best prepared from items just brought in from the market.

For information on the time and place of a market near you, or to find farmers markets while you travel the state, go to www.FarmersMarketsNM.org.

Grilled Vegetable Salad

Peel and slice 1 eggplant. Slice 2 zucchini and 2 yellow squash. Seed and slice 2 green peppers and 2 red peppers.

Coat vegetables in a mixture of ¼ cup vinegar—either red wine or balsamic—and ½ cup olive oil. Season with salt and pepper. Marinate for ½ hour.

Place vegetables in a wire grilling basket and grill over a hot fire until tender, turning until they just begin to char.

Remove from fire, place in a bowl and let cool to room temperature. Taste for seasonings.

Add black or green olives, capers and a teaspoon of good mustard. Mix well.

Serve on a bed of lettuce garnished with cherry tomatoes or as part of an antipasto platter with cheese and salami.

Roasted Farmers Market Salsa

Roast 3 ears of corn and let cool. Remove kernels from cobs.

Peel and seed 3–4 meaty green chiles.

Finely chop 2 large tomatoes.

Mince 3 cloves garlic and 1 small sweet onion. If you like cilantro, add ½ bunch finely chopped.

Dress with the juice of 1 lime, ¼ cup rice vinegar, 1 teaspoon toasted and ground cumin seed, and ½ teaspoon ground red chile. Toss well and serve with a basket of blue corn chips.

This salsa, however, is not for blue corn chips only. It's also great as a topping for a bean burrito, grilled steak, Sunday morning omelette, baked potato with sour cream, or bagel and cream cheese.

Above—*Harvest season is the best time to find handmade decorative arrangements of colorful corn, chile and dried flowers at farmers markets around New Mexico.*

Opposite—*Growers from all over northern New Mexico and southern Colorado get up before dawn to bring their finest produce to the Taos Farmers Market.*

Above—*Keeping the farm running requires the efforts of several generations. An array of homemade jams, salsas and vegetables tempts buyers at the Taos Farmers Market.*

Left—*In a good season, when orchards have withstood late frosts, roadside vendors in Velarde along N.M. 68 display their famous apples, pears and plums in the fall.*

F airs and festivals offer great opportunities to sample a variety of tasty dishes. I've selected some of the more traditional, popular events to include in this chapter. Attending even a few of them will provide a sure-fire taste of New Mexico. Some, such as the Hatch Chile Festival, celebrate New Mexico's chile harvest, while for others, such as the Albuquerque International Balloon Fiesta, food is just part of the show.

Events come and go, however, and dates may vary with the harvest or the sponsoring organizers, so it is a good idea to check with the local chamber of commerce or visitors' centers before heading out. The annual *New Mexico Vacation Guide*, a free publication from the New Mexico Tourism Department, is another good source of information, as is the Tourism Department Web site (www.newmexico.org).

Public feast days at Indian pueblos provide yet another opportunity to sample the local fry bread and red chile. The Indian Pueblo Cultural Center in Albuquerque provides up-to-date lists of such events, which include traditional dancing and offer the opportunity to purchase pottery and other handmade goods, often from the artists themselves. Still, be aware that tribal events may be canceled due to unforeseen circumstances such as a death in the village, so it's always wise to call the pueblo's governor's office first.

Fairs and rodeos on the Navajo and Apache reservations also offer delicious Native dishes.

Numerous wine festivals, featuring tastings of New Mexico vintages, are sponsored through the New Mexico Wine Growers Association. Artists'

Above—*Sunflowers bloom in the fields at Rainbow Ranch in Folsom. Check newspapers for announcements of farm tours in the summer and fall around New Mexico.*

Opposite—*Young dancers participate in a summer folk festival at the Millicent Rogers Museum in Taos.*

studio tours, generally beginning in the spring and continuing into the fall, are another fine way to sample homemade regional dishes. Farm tours, scheduled occasionally in places such as Abiquiú and the Taos area, bring you into the fields.

Some of the best barbecue around may be found at county fairs, such as the Colfax County Fair, and rodeos. Keep your eye out for Dutch-oven cook-offs. Many small towns celebrate the Fourth of July in high style with parades, vendors and fireworks. Some communities offer festive Cinco de Mayo events where you can hear mariachi music while tasting some of the state's spiciest dishes.

Many festivals are naturally associated with the harvest season. New Mexico now boasts several Oktoberfest events, complete with locally brewed beers and oompah bands.

The holiday season is sure to find you with a bowl of posole, *bizcochitos* and tamales to warm your heart and soul.

This list of events is not inclusive by any means, so be prepared to add your own entries as you venture through the state.

January
Ice Fishing Tournament and Chile Dinner, Eagle Nest
Taos Winter Wine Festival, Taos Ski Valley
Hispano Chamber Matanza, Belén

February
Cuchillo Pecan Festival, Cuchillo
ARTfeast, Santa Fe
Mardi Gras in the Clouds, Cloudcroft

March
Fiery Foods and BBQ Festival, Albuquerque

April
Gathering of Nations Powwow, Albuquerque
Chuck Wagon Cook-Off, Ute Lake State Park, Tucumcari

May
Mescal Roast and Mountain Spirit Dance, Living Desert
    State Park, Carlsbad
Southern New Mexico Wine Festival, Las Cruces
Bernalillo Wine Festival

June
High Rolls Cherry Festival, High Rolls
Dairy Fest, Clovis
Elephant Butte Chili Challenge Cook-Off

July

N.M. Pork & Brew State Barbecue Championship, Rio Rancho

Fourth of July celebrations—Eagle Nest and Raton have two of
the best

Old-Timers' Reunion, Magdalena

Lavender in the Village, Los Ranchos de Albuquerque

Taos Powwow

August

Santa Fe Indian Market

Gallup Inter-Tribal Ceremonial

Cimarrón Days

Sunflower Festival, Mountainair

Fiesta de San Lorenzo, Bernalillo

September

New Mexico Wine Festival, Bernalillo

Pie Town Festival, Pie Town

Santa Fe Fiesta

Hatch Chile Festival, Hatch

Bean Day, Wagon Mound

New Mexico State Fair, Albuquerque

Raspberry Festival, Salman Raspberry Ranch, La Cueva

Clovis Music Festival

Corrales Harvest Festival

Whole Enchilada Festival, Las Cruces
Sabor de Las Vegas
Cleveland Roller Millfest
Chile Cheese Festival, Roswell
Santa Fe Wine & Chile Fiesta, Santa Fe
Solanofest Dutch Oven Cook-off, Harding County
Harvest Wine Festival, Southern New Mexico State Fairgrounds

October

Albuquerque International Balloon Fiesta
Lincoln County Cowboy Symposium, Ruidoso
Oktoberfest, in Alamogordo, Aztec, Socorro, Red River and Rio
     Rancho
Shiprock (Navajo) Fair
New Mexico Pumpkin Festival, Las Cruces
Pinto Bean Fiesta, Moriarty
Peanut Valley Festival, Portales

November

Dixon Artists Studio Tour
Día de los Muertos, Mesilla

December

Farolito walks and *luminaria* tours
Pueblo Indian dances